Confiscation Measures and Sanctions in Corruption Cases in Kazakhstan

OECD

BETTER POLICIES FOR BETTER LIVES

This work is published under the responsibility of the Secretary-General of the OECD. The opinions expressed and arguments employed herein do not necessarily reflect the official views of the Member countries of the OECD.

This document, as well as any data and map included herein, are without prejudice to the status of or sovereignty over any territory, to the delimitation of international frontiers and boundaries and to the name of any territory, city or area.

Please cite this publication as:
OECD (2025), *Confiscation Measures and Sanctions in Corruption Cases in Kazakhstan*, OECD Publishing, Paris, https://doi.org/10.1787/60159d3f-en.

ISBN 978-92-64-59782-2 (print)
ISBN 978-92-64-80379-4 (PDF)
ISBN 978-92-64-78557-1 (HTML)

Photo credits: Cover © janetheone/Getty Images Plus.

Corrigenda to OECD publications may be found at: https://www.oecd.org/en/publications/support/corrigenda.html.

Foreword

This report explores the application of confiscation measures in Kazakhstan, with a particular focus on the legal framework, judicial practice and high-level corruption cases. It analyses the practice of applying confiscation measures, judicial sanctions, statutes of limitations, and procedural immunities for public officials against investigative enforcement steps, identifying shortcomings and gaps in these areas. The report also includes recommendations for amendments in the legislation, and for reinforcing law enforcement and judicial practice. These recommendations are intended to facilitate Kazakhstan's progress in improving its confiscation framework and its implementation by proposing appropriate solutions to identified weaknesses and gaps.

The report comprises recommendations for further policy improvements and practice development that can be utilised by Kazakh authorities for improving the application of preventive and reparative confiscation measures and effective, proportionate and dissuasive sanctions in corruption cases by the state. These recommendations are non–mandatory, nevertheless, the authorities are expected to develop an action plan for addressing identified gaps and shortcomings.

The report was prepared by Vitaliy Kasko and Maris Urbans under the country-specific anti-corruption project for Kazakhstan funded by the U.S. Department of State's Bureau of International Narcotics and Law Enforcement Affairs and implemented by the Anti-Corruption Network for Eastern Europe and Central Asia (ACN) – a regional outreach programme of the Organisation for Economic Co-operation and Development (OECD) Working Group on Bribery.

The report benefited from the input from the Anti-Corruption and Integrity in Government Division of the Public Governance Directorate: Elena Konceviciute, Global Relations and Co-operation Directorate/EURASIA: Celeste Laporte Talamon and Vakulik Mariia, and Anti-Corruption Division of the Directorate for Financial and Enterprise Affairs: Marion Barraclough.

Gratitude for the helpful support with the formatting, design, and promotion of this report of the study extends to Genieve Crump, Liv Gudmundson and Flora Monsaingeon-Lavuri, Communications Officers. The authors express their gratitude to the ACN's National Co-ordinators and other stakeholders in Kazakhstan for their input.

Table of contents

TABLES

BOXES

Abbreviations

ACN	Anti-corruption network for Eastern Europe and Central Asia
CC	Criminal Code of the Republic of Kazakhstan
CE	Council of Europe
CPC	Criminal Procedure Code of the Republic of Kazakhstan
EU	European Union
EUR	Euro
GRECO	Group of States Against Corruption
IAP	Istanbul Anti-Corruption Action Plan
KZT	Kazakhstani tenge
LLP	Limited liability partnership
MCI	Monthly calculation indicators
NGO	Non-governmental organisation
OECD	Organisation for Economic Co-operation and Development
RK	Republic of Kazakhstan
UNCAC	United Nations Convention Against Corruption
USD	United States dollar

Executive summary

Corruption deepens inequality and weakens economic growth, as well as reduces trust in government, undermining the sustainability and proper functioning of the democratic foundations of society and the state. Corruption is estimated to cost the European Union between EUR 179 billion and EUR 990 billion per year, accounting for up to 6% of its GDP (European Union, 2023[1]). Corruption is committed primarily for economic gain, and allows corrupt public officials, their relatives and affiliates to supplement their wealth with public funds.

The fight against corruption is a multifaceted challenge, requiring robust legal frameworks, effective enforcement and sanctioning mechanisms. Confiscation of profits gained through criminal activity is one of the most effective tools and strategies for tackling corruption offenses. It not only ensures that no one benefits from criminal activities and provides justice for the wronged party; it also discourages individuals and companies from engaging in corrupt activities, particularly when penalties are effective, proportionate and dissuasive, are consistently enforced and are made public.

Improving the implementation of confiscation measures is an important step towards a more comprehensive and effective approach to dealing with corruption offenses. In a recent report, the OECD recognised that enhancing national confiscation regimes is a complex issue (OECD, 2024[2]), though comprehensive and efficient regimes have an important role in countering corruption offenses.

Several international legal instruments, such as the United Nations Convention Against Corruption (UNCAC) (2004[3]) and Directive 2014/42/EU of the European Parliament and of the Council of 3 April 2014 on the freezing and confiscation of instruments and proceeds of crime in the European Union (European Union, 2014[4]) set standards and best practices in this area. These include the direct confiscation of instruments and proceeds from corruption crimes, as well as the seizure and confiscation of criminal proceeds transformed into derivative property, commingled with legal assets, and registered or transferred to informed third parties. Modern confiscation tools include value-based, extended and non-conviction-based confiscation regimes. Investigations and prosecutions of corruption offenses may encounter legal challenges, such as keeping up with the period of limitations or necessity to seek the lifting of the immunity against prosecution. Both legal concepts assure fair legal processes and protect individual rights within the judicial system, though they need to be balanced with any legal limitations placed on law enforcement to not cause unreasonable impediments to investigating and prosecuting corruption.

In recent years, Kazakhstan has taken steps to reinforce its confiscation regime by enhancing available confiscation tools, which includes introducing a legal framework for civil confiscation. However, there is still substantial potential for improving the relevant legislative framework. Improvements can still be made to confiscation practices under the current confiscation regime, which would contribute to making the implementation of confiscation measures more effective.

The report advocates for a reform of Kazakhstan's confiscation framework to strengthen anti-corruption efforts. The key recommendations focus on shifting from the current hybrid model to a more robust and clear legal structure that emphasizes both the confiscation of instruments and proceeds from criminal activities, distinct from material evidence. It underscores the need for legislation to explicitly define and treat assets such as instruments (tools and means) of committing crimes as mandatory objects of confiscation, ensuring consistency across all corruption offenses. Moreover, it is recommended that Kazakhstan clearly differentiates between the confiscation of material evidence and the confiscation of proceeds from crime, thereby streamlining law enforcement and judicial processes.

Further, the report emphasizes the importance of enhancing the capacity of investigators, prosecutors, and judges involved in corruption cases through targeted training aligned with the new confiscation model. It suggests that proceedings for non-conviction-based confiscation should be conducted independently of the underlying criminal case, advocating for a "balance of probabilities" standard of proof to facilitate asset confiscation, including assets held in third-party names. This approach aims to broaden the scope of assets subject to confiscation and strengthen enforcement.

In terms of investigative practices, the report highlights the importance of systematically identifying and confiscating instruments and proceeds during investigations. It recommends shifting the focus from damages caused by corruption to the proceeds from corruption offenses itself, providing a more effective basis for confiscation. The confiscation framework should also extend to mixed proceeds and clarify procedures for confiscating assets from informed third parties, ensuring sufficient protection of property rights of bona fide owners. The introduction of extended confiscation measures, inspired by European Union directives, is suggested as a way to enhance asset recovery efforts.

The report stresses the need for stricter sentencing guidelines for severe corruption offenses, advocating for mandatory custodial sentences and the exemption of such offenses from leniency provisions unless justified by exceptional circumstances. It also recommends introducing corporate criminal liability for corruption.

Finally, the current system for collecting and analysing confiscation data requires improvement; collected data should specify the types, values, and total amounts of assets confiscated to enable better monitoring and policy development. Overall, these reforms aim to make Kazakhstan's anti-corruption measures more effective, transparent, and aligned with international best practices.

1 Recommendations

The chapter summarises the key recommendations of this report, which focus on seven overarching areas, including confiscation frameworks, capacity building and specialisation, statistics, pre-trial confiscation, penalties, lifting immunities and statutes of limitations, and accessibility of court verdicts.

Confiscation framework

- Bring the legal framework for criminal confiscation into full compliance with international standards, in particular, UNCAC (2004[3]) a and best practices in the region by ensuring a transition from the existing hybrid model of confiscation as a sanction to that of confiscation of instruments (tools and means) of a crime, proceeds of criminal offenses and any benefit therefrom (as a criminal law measure other than a sanction).
- Before the implementation of the above recommended reform of the framework for criminal confiscation, as an interim measure, exclude all corruption offenses from the scope of application of Part 4 of Article 55 of the CC (2014[5]) by supplementing the list of relevant offenses in Part 8 of Article 55 of the CC.
- Ensure that the revised framework for confiscation of instruments, proceeds and benefits of criminal offenses applies to all corruption-related criminal offenses without exception (including corruption in the private sector).
- Make a clear distinction between the objects of the updated confiscation model and the concept of material evidence to eliminate overlaps and challenges with law enforcement in practice (ensuring that the confiscation of instruments, proceeds and benefits of corruption and other proceeds-generating crimes that have material value are prioritised).
- Include in the law detailed provisions on the criminal confiscation of property belonging to informed third parties (both individuals and legal entities). These provisions should include clear criteria for applying such confiscation and appropriate safeguards to protect the rights of genuine third parties.
- Formalise the concept of "instruments, tools, and means of committing a crime" as a mandatory object for confiscation, while ensuring a clear distinction between their confiscation and the disposition of material evidence.
- Formalise the concept of “proceeds from crime”—including direct and derivative proceeds, as well as any subsequent profits and benefits derived from them—as mandatory objects for confiscation, provided there is a proven link to the specific crime through which they were obtained. Additionally, ensure their confiscation is distinguished from the disposition of material evidence.
- Ensure that, during the prosecution of corruption offenses, instruments (tools and means) used to commit such crimes, direct and derivative proceeds, any subsequent profits and other benefits derived from the commission of corruption offenses are systematically identified, seized, and confiscated in practice, specifically in their capacity as such.
- Ensure a consistent transition in practice from the currently prevailing concept of "damage" from corruption crimes to the conceptualisation of corrupt income or benefits as objects of confiscation in cases of corruption offenses that generate such income or benefits, such as bribery, abuse of power, and embezzlement.
- Provide in legislation for the confiscation of mixed proceeds from crimes as a separate object, aiming to facilitate the confiscation of property corresponding to the assessed value of the associated criminal proceeds, including any subsequent profits and benefits derived therefrom.
- Ensure that during the prosecution of corruption offenses, assets registered in the names of nominal (informed) third parties, including in high-level corruption cases, are systematically identified, seized, and confiscated, while the rights of genuine third parties are upheld in practice.
- Improve the legal framework for criminal non-conviction-based confiscation (Chapter 71 of Section 15 of the Criminal Procedure Code (CPC) (2014[6])). This can be achieved by ensuring the autonomy of this process from the primary investigation. The relevant steps may include

establishing a lighter burden of proof, limiting the elements to be proven, broadening the range of objects of confiscation (including instruments, direct and indirect proceeds from crimes, mixed proceeds, equivalents, etc.), ensuring effective confiscation of assets registered to informed third parties, and enhancing the right to protection for individuals whose property is considered for confiscation.

- Introduce the framework for extended criminal confiscation into the legislation of Kazakhstan based on the provisions of Directive (EU) 2024/1260 (2024[7]) regarding asset recovery and confiscation, as well as best practices from countries in the region.
- Establish an aggravated form of bribery (active and passive) in the CC (2014[5]) when this is committed by a person holding a responsible public position.
- Ensure that all serious and especially serious corruption offenses, particularly high-level corruption, are subject to custodial sentences of imprisonment that are non-optional, with durations sufficient to ensure their effectiveness, proportionality, and deterrent impact. Fines (multiples of the amount of the bribe or other form of corrupt benefit, or fines in a certain amount) may be an additional penalty (in addition to non-alternative sanctions of imprisonment) for serious and especially serious corruption offenses rather than an alternative to them. Fines could also be an additional penalty for other types of corruption offenses (of minor or medium) rather than the principal penalty for them.
- Exclude all corruption offenses from the scope of Part 2 and Part 3 of Article 56 of the CC (2014[5]) (imposing punishment for an incomplete crime). Exclude all bribery offenses from the scope of Part 2 and 3 of Article 56 of the CC or criminalise the offer and promise of a bribe, as well as the acceptance of an offer or promise of a bribe as a completed offense (for bribery in both the public and private sectors).
- Exclude corruption offenses from the scope of Part 1 of Article 55 of the CC (2014[5]) (imposition of a more lenient punishment than is provided for this criminal offense) and the scope of Part 4 of Article 55 of the CC, supplementing the exceptions in Part 8 of Article 55 of the CC with a reference to corruption offenses.
- Exclude corruption offenses from the scope of Article 72 of the CC (2014[5]) (parole from serving a sentence) or further limit the scope of its application to exceptional cases that are clearly formulated.
- Exclude corruption offenses from the scope of Article 73 of the CC (2014[5]) (substitution of the unexecuted part of the sentence with a more lenient type of punishment or a reduction of the sentence).
- Introduce the liability of legal entities for corruption offenses in legislation based on international standards and best practices in the region, establishing effective, proportionate and dissuasive criminal sanctions for such legal entities, including financial sanctions.
- Implement measures to ensure that property seizure and confiscation are systematically and consistently applied in practice in cases of corruption offenses involving illicit income.

Capacity building and specialisation

- Make it a priority for investigators and prosecutors to fully pursue the confiscation of proceeds of corruption (or their equivalents), particularly in cases of high-level corruption.
- Consider introducing a specialisation for investigators and prosecutors focused exclusively on financial investigations, asset detection and recovery in corruption cases, particularly of high-level corruption.
- Enhance the capacity of investigators, prosecutors, and judges specialising in the prosecution and judicial review of corruption cases, ensuring that the confiscation of property (the value of which

corresponds to the value of direct and indirect proceeds from corruption offenses), is systematically applied in practice.

Statistics

- Improve keeping the statistics on criminal confiscations by including detailed data that distinguishes between types of criminal confiscations and objects of confiscation measures, including confiscation from third parties (natural and legal persons). This should include differentiating between the types and levels of officials subject to confiscation measures, as well as the types of corrupt benefits obtained and confiscated. Additionally, include data on the amounts or value of assets subject to court confiscation orders and the total funds received by the budget as a result of these confiscations.
- Ensure that detailed statistics on criminal confiscation in corruption cases, including high-level corruption, are published periodically (at least annually) to guarantee transparency and accessibility for the public.
- Ensure that official statistics clearly identify the number of persons whose criminal cases were terminated on the basis of Para 4 of Part 1 of Article 35 of CPC (due to the expiration of the statute of limitations for bringing to criminal responsibility), and the number of those who belonged to the category of public officials.
- Ensure that judicial statistics on corruption offenses include data on the types of penalties imposed by courts on different categories of officials (i.e., a breakdown by level and type of official on whom certain penalties are imposed).

Criminal non-conviction-based confiscation

- Ensure the autonomy of criminal non-conviction-based confiscation proceedings (Chapter 71 of Section 15 of CPC (2014[6])) so that they do not depend directly and automatically on the progress and outcomes of the primary criminal proceedings. The termination of the case against the individual or their acquittal in the primary proceedings should not entail the automatic cancellation of confiscation within the criminal non-conviction-based confiscation.
- Ensure that the legal framework for criminal non-conviction-based confiscation covers a broad range of objects, including instruments (tools and means) of the crime, proceeds from crimes, profits or other benefits derived from them, commingled proceeds, and value-based confiscation.
- Apply the criminal non-conviction-based confiscation framework effectively to assets registered in the names of informed third parties, without the necessity of resorting to legal remedies such as the annulment of transactions in civil proceedings.

Penalties

- Ensure, through effective, proportionate and dissuasive criminal sanctions, that high-level corruption offenses (in terms of the level of the public official's position and/or the size of the corrupt benefit) are always categorised as serious or particularly serious offenses, including corruption in the private sector (under the criteria of the size of the corrupt benefit).

Lifting Immunities and statutes of limitations

- Consider amending legislation to permit review of decisions to terminate criminal cases due to refusal to lift immunity when relevant circumstances change, such as the loss of immunity entitlement or changes in the body authorised to lift immunity. Additionally, allow for submitting a repeated application to lift immunity based on new arguments or evidence. Lastly, include provisions to suspend the statute of limitations during these review processes to ensure timely prosecution.
- Consider re-including corruption offenses in the list of crimes specified in Part 6 of Article 71 of the CC (2014[5]), to which the statute of limitations on criminal liability does not apply. Additionally, consider adding the offense of legalization (laundering) of proceeds from corruption. Alternatively, consider expanding the grounds for suspending the statute of limitations in criminal cases by establishing that suspension applies at any stage of the proceedings prior to the entry into legal force of the judgment. This could include periods from the initiation of criminal proceedings, the suspicion or accusation of a suspect, or the referral of the case to court for indictment, among others.
- Ensure implementation of the recommendations of the Report of the Fourth Round of Monitoring under the IAP (OECD, 2017[8]) and address the shortcomings noted in the Baseline Report of the Fifth Round of Monitoring of Anti-Corruption Reforms in Kazakhstan under the IAP (OECD, 2024[9]) regarding immunities, in particular, ensure that general immunities are replaced by functional immunities, substantially reduce the number of public officials with immunities and procedural limitations on immunities.
- Ensure that official statistics include data on the number of applications to lift immunity from public officials and the outcomes of their consideration. Additionally, record the number of criminal case terminations under Para 10 of Part 1 of Article 35 of CPC, with a breakdown by level and type of officials, and make this information publicly accessible.

Accessibility of judicial rulings

- Enhance the public segment of the court verdicts database to enable searches for verdicts and other court decisions in criminal cases based on various criteria. These criteria may include crime categories, articles of the CC (2014[5]), keywords, the date of the ruling, and other relevant parameters.

2 Types of confiscation

The chapter focuses on the legal framework for confiscation in Kazakhstan. It covers three types of available confiscation regimes applicable to corruption related assets, particularly, special confiscation, confiscation in pre-trial stage of investigation and civil confiscation, providing its assessment against relevant international standards.

Confiscation of property in criminal cases, including criminal cases on corruption offenses, is governed by the CC (2014[5]) and CPC (2014[6]). Additionally, civil confiscation, which does not require a criminal conviction, is regulated in the Law "On the Return of Illegally Acquired Assets to the State" (Republic of Kazakhstan, 2023[10]).

2.1 Special confiscation

The CC (2014[5]) in Para 1, part 3, article 40 provides that confiscation of property may be applied to a person found guilty of committing a criminal offense, in addition to the principal penalty.

According to Article 48 of the CC (2014[5]), confiscation of property is the compulsory seizure and acquisition by the state of property owned by the convicted person, obtained by criminal means or acquired with funds obtained by criminal means, or property that is tools or means of committing a criminal offense.

The following property (including money) can be confiscated:

- property received as a result of the commission of a criminal offense, and any proceeds from that property, except for property and proceeds therefrom to be returned to the lawful owner,
- property that results from partial or complete transformation or conversion of property obtained as a result of the commission of a criminal offense and the proceeds of that property,
- property used or intended for financing or other provision of extremist or terrorist activity or criminal group,
- property being an instrument or means of committing a criminal offense,
- property specified in Paras 1, 2, 3 and 4 above, transferred by the convicted person to the property of other persons (part 2 of Article 48 of the CC).

If confiscation of a certain item included in the above-mentioned property is impossible at the time of the court's decision due to the item's consumption, sale or other reason, the court shall confiscate a sum of money that corresponds to the value of this item (part 3 of Article 48 of the CC). However, according to part 5 of Article 48 of the CC, the following two types of property are not subject to confiscation:

1) property necessary for the convicted person or persons dependent on him/her, according to the list provided for by the penal enforcement legislation,

2) funds and other property legalised in accordance with the Law of the Republic of Kazakhstan “On the Amnesty of Citizens of the Republic of Kazakhstan, Oralmans,[1] and Persons Holding Residence Permits in the Republic of Kazakhstan, in Connection with the Legalisation of Their Property,” insofar as assets were acquired as a result of committing a criminal offense for which the same Law provides an exemption from criminal liability. The latter provisions do not apply to judicial acts that became final as of 1 September 2014, and do not extend to laundered property and funds that were not subject to legalisation under the law.

Numerous articles of the CC provide for confiscation as a mandatory or an optional additional punishment for a crime. In the latter case, legal provisions include the following wording: “with or without confiscation of property”. However, the law does not provide a guidance on the circumstances under which additional penalties should be applied. In such cases, the application of confiscation remains at the absolute discretion of the court.

Exceptions to the application of criminal confiscation

The current criminal legislation of Kazakhstan provides that in some cases, the court has discretion to not impose confiscation as an additional punishment at all, even if confiscation is mandatory under the relevant criminal offense.

Thus, in accordance with part 4 of article 55 of the CC (2014[5]), the court may impose punishment below the lowest limit under the relevant article of the CC, or the court may either impose a penalty that is more lenient than that provided for in the relevant article of the CC, or not impose an additional sanction that under the relevant law would usually be mandatory. Such court`s discretion is applicable if there are exceptional circumstances related to the goals and motives of the act, the role of the perpetrator, their behaviour during or after the commission of the criminal offense, or other circumstances that significantly reduce the degree of public danger of the wrongdoing. Additionally, it applies in cases where a participant in a criminal offense actively assists in disclosing the acts committed by their accomplices.

Both individual mitigating circumstances and an aggregate of such circumstances may be recognised as exceptional (Part 5 of Article 55 of the CC (2014[5])). This rule is not applicable to types of offenses (Part 8 of Article 55). Corruption offenses are not included in the list of non-applicability. Such legislative regulation effectively nullifies the mandatory application of confiscation of instruments (tools and means of commission), proceeds from crimes (including corruption), and any benefits derived from them, making the application of confiscation directly dependent on the discretion of the court in each specific case, based on part 4 of Article 55 of the CC.

All corruption offenses in the public sector (as provided by UNCAC (United Nations, 2004[3])) are subject to mandatory confiscation as an additional punishment.

These offenses are misappropriation or embezzlement of entrusted property committed by a public official (Parts 2-4 of Article 189 of the CC), abuse of official powers (Article 361 of the CC), taking a bribe (Article 366 of the CC), giving a bribe (Article 367 of the CC), mediation in bribery (Article 368 of the CC), as well as legalisation (laundering) of money and/or other property obtained by criminal means (Article 218 of the CC).

By contrast, criminal offenses for corruption in the private sector, for example, commercial bribery (Part 1, Article 253 of the CC (2014[5])) do not always provide for confiscation as an additional penalty. For some offenses, confiscation is optional at the discretion of the court (for example, abuse of authority (Articles 250 and 251 of the CC). Thus, the current criminal legislation essentially allows that in the case of a number of corruption offenses committed in the private sector, confiscation under Article 48 of the CC (instruments, means of commission and proceeds of such crimes) may not be imposed, being at the discretion of the court, or is not available at all (Part 1, Article 253 of the CC).

Article 118 of CPC (2014[6]) specifically addresses the recognition of certain items and property as material evidence, along with the rules for handling material evidence during the termination of criminal proceedings or in sentencing decisions. Some types of material evidence essentially duplicate the subject of confiscation as a punishment under Article 48 of the CC (2014[5]). According to part 1 of Article 118 of CPC, the following shall be recognised as material evidence:

- objects, if there is reason to believe that they served as an instrument or other means of committing a criminal offense (Para. 1),
- items that were the objects of socially dangerous encroachment (Para. 3),
- money, valuables and other property obtained as a result of committing a criminal offense (Para. 4),

In accordance with Part 3 of Article 118 of CPC (2014[6]), the decision on further disposition with material evidence must be taken when deciding on the termination of a criminal case or passing a sentence, according to the following rules:

- Instruments and means of committing a criminal offense belonging to the perpetrator shall be subject to confiscation on the basis of Article 48 of the CC (2014[5]).
- Instruments and means of committing a criminal offense, lawfully belonging to a person who did not know or should not have known of the unlawful purpose of using his property, shall be returned to that person.
- In other cases, the instruments and means of committing a criminal offense shall be transferred to appropriate institutions, to certain persons or destroyed.
- Things prohibited for circulation or restricted in circulation shall be transferred to appropriate institutions or destroyed.
- Money and other property obtained by criminal means or acquired with funds obtained by criminal means, with the exception of property and proceeds therefrom, are subject to return to the lawful owner, shall by court decision be subject to conversion to the revenue of the state; the remaining things shall be given to the lawful owners and, if the latter are not identified, shall become the property of the state. The remaining items shall be handed over to their lawful owners and, if the latter are not identified, shall become the property of the State. In the event of a dispute as to the ownership of these things, the dispute shall be resolved by civil proceedings.

Article 118 of CPC (2014[6]) mirrors the provisions of Article 48 of the CC (2014[5]), as both address the confiscation of money and other assets acquired through criminal means, as well as the instruments and means used to commit a criminal offense. However, there are notable differences in their regulations. For instance, according to Para 5 of Part 2 of Article 48 of the CC, instruments and means of committing a crime that are transferred by the convicted person to the ownership of others are subject to confiscation. In contrast, Para 1-1 of Part 3 of Article 118 of CPC stipulates that instruments and means of committing a crime that are legally owned by someone who did not know, or should not have known, about the unlawful purposes of the property are to be returned to that person.

Additionally, both norms do not clarify the actions required for property used as instruments or means of committing a crime that belongs to a person who knew, or should have known, about its unlawful use. There are also differences in how the proceeds of crime and the conditions for their confiscation (as stated in Article 48 of the CC (2014[5])) or transfer to the state (as outlined in Article 118 of CPC) are described in Part 2 of Article 48 of the CC and Part 3 of Article 118 of CPC.

Analysis of compliance with international standards

Existing regime of criminal confiscation of instruments of corruption, proceeds of crime and any benefit from them does not fully comply with international standards and have potential for improvement by learning from the best practices across the ACN region.

The existing confiscation model in the Kazakhstan has been repeatedly criticised in the reports of international organisations. Thus, the Fourth monitoring round report on Kazakhstan under the IAP, notes that although it is not explicitly stated in the General Part of CC (2014[5]), based on the provisions of the Special Part, confiscation will be applied in cases specified in the relevant articles of the Special Part of the CC. Mandatory confiscation is provided for many, but not all corruption offenses. The Round 3 Report also questioned the validity of establishing confiscation as a criminal sanction. In particular, the international standard is mandatory confiscation of criminally acquired property, as well as of property that is an instrument or means of committing a criminal offense. Along with the lack of full coverage of all *corpus delicti* of corruption offenses, the inclusion of confiscation of criminally obtained property, as well as instruments and means of committing crimes in the system of punishment, gives the courts unreasonably broad discretionary powers [according to the provisions of Article 55 of the CC, which allow courts not to impose confiscation as an additional punishment]. Under such circumstances, confiscation of instruments and means of crime, as well as criminal proceeds provided for by the CC cannot be considered as unconditional in a broad sense. Group of States Against Corruption (GRECO) Joint First and Second Rounds Evaluation Report on Kazakhstan (GRECO, 2022[11]) states that confiscation of property is explicitly provided for in the CC as a sanction for certain corruption-related offenses. However, the application of confiscation for these offenses is not mandatory but is a discretion of the court.

Given the above, it is advisable to reform Kazakhstan's criminal confiscation system in order to shift from the existing hybrid system of confiscation as a sanction (additional punishment) to confiscation of instruments of and proceeds from criminal offenses and any benefit therefrom (as a measure of criminal-legal enforcement, a measure of criminal law nature or a similar legal concept of criminal law other than a sanction). As a priority interim measure, all corruption offenses should be excluded from the scope of Part 4 of Article 55 of the CC (2014[5]), which provides for the discretionary right of the court not to apply the existing confiscation measure as an additional punishment for the crime.

It is also recommended that legislation should ensure that confiscation of instruments and proceeds of crime and any benefit derived therefrom should be extended to all corruption criminal offenses in their international legal sense without exception (including criminal offenses for corruption in the private sector).

Additionally, a clear distinction should be made between the objects of such an updated confiscation model and material evidence in order to eliminate duplication of these concepts and challenges with their enforcement in practice. Furthermore, if the property in the case was an instrumentality or proceeds of crime or any benefit from it that has material value, it should be subject to seizure and confiscation as such, while all other items (not captured by instruments, proceeds and benefits of crime that have material value) may fall under the legal framework for material evidence on a residual principle (other property, items, documents that may serve as means for the detection of a crime, establishment of the factual circumstances of the case, identification of offenders, refutation of their guilt, or mitigation of their liability).

2.2 Confiscation during the pre-trial investigation

Non-conviction-based confiscation is an important tool in the fight against corruption, organised crime, and other serious offenses. In its various forms, it provides authorities with advanced means to ensure that offenders and their accomplices do not benefit from criminal activities, even in cases where obtaining a conviction is not possible. This tool allows authorities to confiscate assets for which there are reasonable suspicions of a connection to criminal activity, without waiting for a criminal conviction. This is particularly useful in cases where the offender is unavailable (has fled, died, etc.). Furthermore, by potentially increasing the risks associated with asset confiscation, non-conviction-based confiscation serves as a deterrent to criminal behaviour, complicating individuals' engagement in illegal activities with the awareness that their assets may be subject to confiscation even in the absence of a conviction.

There are three main models of this type of confiscation used by countries:

- The classical model covers situations where the defendant in a criminal process has been established, but the criminal proceedings cannot be concluded with a conviction due to reasons such as death, absconding, evasion of justice in another country, amnesty, expiration of the statute of limitations for criminal liability, etc.
- The property-targeted (in rem) model focuses on the assets rather than the individual, aiming at restitution or prevention of criminal activity without requiring the conviction of an individual for the predicate offense. Such proceedings are generally civil in nature, and there is no need to demonstrate a connection between the targeted assets and a specific criminal act. However, in most national legal systems of this kind, the state must still demonstrate at least an indirect link of such assets to criminal activity in a broad sense, for example, in connection with involvement in organised crime or a relation to a person engaged in such criminal activity.

- The non-conviction-based model does not require any connection (direct or indirect) to a specific predicate crime or criminal activity in a broad sense. It only requires demonstrating a difference (usually substantial) between an individual's assets and their lawful income (unjustified wealth).

Chapter 71 of Section 15 of CPC outlines the procedure for confiscating property obtained through criminal means in pre-trial stage.

In accordance with the provisions of Article 667 of CPC (2014[6]), in cases, where a suspect or accused person (in ongoing criminal proceedings) is declared internationally wanted, or where criminal prosecution against them is terminated based on Paras 3, 4 and 11 of Part 1 of Article 35 of CPC (due to an amnesty act, due to the expiry of the statute of limitations, due to death of a defendant), the official, conducting the pre-trial investigation, upon obtaining information about property acquired unlawfully, shall initiate (separate) confiscation proceedings.

The person conducting the pre-trial investigation shall issue a decision to allocate materials for the confiscation proceedings. This decision will include copies of the materials from the criminal case related to the offense that serves as the basis for the confiscation, as well as the supporting evidence specified in part three of Article 113 of CPC (2014[6]) (essentially, all files necessary for consideration of the guilt or innocence of the defendant in the criminal case).

In proceedings on confiscation without a conviction, in addition to the circumstances provided for in Paras 1 and 3 of Article 113 of CPC[2] (2014[6]), the following must be proven:

- ownership of the property by a suspect, an accused or a third person,
- a link between the property and the offense that is the basis for the application of confiscation,
- circumstances under which property was acquired by a third party or that give rise to the belief that the property was acquired as a result of an infringement.

In the event that circumstances are established indicating that the suspect or accused is concealing property by transferring it to other persons, the individual conducting the pre-trial investigation shall apply to the prosecutor with a request to file a petition with the court in the interests of the state or the victims in the criminal case, seeking the annulment of transactions (such as sales, gifts, leases, fiduciary management, and others) in accordance with civil proceedings (Parts 2 and 3 of Article 668 of CPC).

Upon recognizing that sufficient evidence has been gathered in non-conviction-based confiscation proceedings that the assets were obtained illegally, the person conducting the pre-trial investigation drafts a relevant opinion, which, together with the files, is forwarded to the prosecutor. The prosecutor, having considered the opinion, shall file a petition for confiscation with the court having jurisdiction over the criminal case on the offense investigated by the criminal prosecution body. If there are no grounds for filing a petition with the court, the prosecutor shall return the opinion and materials to the person conducting the pre-trial investigation with an instruction to collect additional evidence or to terminate the confiscation proceedings. The procedure is carried out by the prosecutor within 10 days (Paras 4-8 of Article 668 of CPC (2014[6]).

The petition on application of non-conviction-based confiscation is decided by a judge sitting alone. If examination of additional materials is necessary, a judge has the right to request the files of a criminal case. The prosecutor who filed the petition participates in the court hearing. At the request of the defence attorney of the suspect or accused, if it is present at the hearing, other individuals may be summoned to give testimony. Following the consideration of the petition for confiscation, the court issues a ruling, resolving the following questions:

- Is the property of the suspect or accused linked to the crime that serves as the basis for confiscation under Article 48 of the CC (2014[5])?
- Was the property of a third party acquired in a manner provided for by Article 48 of the CC?

- Is confiscation applicable, and to what portion of the property should it be applied?
- What should be done with the frozen or seized property that is not subject to confiscation?
- What are the costs incurred in the confiscation proceedings, and to whom are they allocated (Articles 669 and 670 of CPC (2014[6]))?

As a result of a pre-trial confiscation proceedings, the court shall render one of the following rulings:

- granting the application and confiscating the property, or
- denying the application for confiscation.

A copy of such a ruling is served on the prosecutor and other participants in the proceedings or mailed to those participants who did not participate in the proceedings. A copy of the ruling is also delivered to the person from whom the property is confiscated. After the ruling enters into legal force, the court that issued the ruling sends the writ of execution, a copy of the inventory of property and a copy of the ruling to the relevant justice authority for execution in accordance with the procedure established for the execution of confiscation sentences. A confiscation ruling may be appealed by the defence or reviewed at the request of the prosecutor in the manner prescribed by the law (Articles 671 and 672 of CPC (2014[6])).

The institution of non-conviction-based confiscation, provided for in Chapter 71 of CPC, has previously received generally favourable assessments in reports of international organisations, with some reservations. Thus, the Report of the 4th Round of Monitoring of Anti-Corruption Reforms in Kazakhstan (OECD, 2017[8]) noted that the provisions on non-conviction-based confiscation are progressive and in line with international best practices and standards, e.g., the Directive 2014/42/EU on the freezing and confiscation of instruments and proceeds of crime in the European Union (2014[4]). At the same time, safeguards to protect the rightful interests of the person, whose property is confiscated prior to conviction, should be enhanced. In particular, it should be stipulated that the defence counsel of a defendant must be summoned to the court hearing (at the same time, the non-appearance of these persons, if they have been duly notified, should not prevent the court proceedings and consideration of the confiscation application). Additionally, the GRECO (2022[11]) recognises the procedure under Chapter 71 of CPC (2014[6]) as a non-conviction-based criminal confiscation.

2.3 Confiscation in civil proceedings

On 12 July 2023, Kazakhstan adopted the Law "On the Return of Illegally Acquired Assets to the State" (2023[10]). According to the Law, assets are considered illegally acquired if they are to be returned to the state due to their classification by a court as assets of unexplained origin, based on the grounds provided in this Law. In turn, assets of unexplained origin are defined in the Law as assets belonging to an individual and/or their affiliated persons, for which the correlation between their value and the amount of lawful income or other legal sources of funding for the acquisition of such assets has not been proven to the court in the manner established by the legislation of Kazakhstan.

The provisions of the Law apply to individuals (subjects) for whom the following information is available:

- the subject under the Law is or was a person holding a responsible state position, a position that implies the performance of managerial functions in a state legal entity or a quasi-state sector entity, and/or has (or had) administrative or authoritative resources (connections, influence) in relation to individuals holding (or who held) responsible state positions, and/or to individuals performing (or who performed) managerial functions in a state legal entity or a quasi-state sector entity,
- the (same) subject under the Law has acquired (whether directly or through affiliated persons, including legal entities) assets, including derivative assets, as a result of utilizing administrative or authoritative resources (also connections, influence), or the same information regarding individuals and legal entities affiliated with the subject under the Law.

A key role in the implementation of the confiscation model it provides is attributed to the Commission and the Authorised body for the return of assets. The Commission is a permanent body composed of members of Parliament, public figures, Government members, heads of state bodies and other individuals (the composition of the commission is approved by the Government, and it is headed by the Prime Minister). The commission establishes a Register of subjects whose assets may be subject to confiscation and provides mandatory recommendations to the authorised body for the return of assets (referred to in the Article 1 of the Law as the "working body of the Commission"). The Asset Recovery department of the Prosecutor's Office exercises the functions of the Authorised body. By Presidential Decree dated 5 October 2023, the Committee for the Recovery of Assets of the General Prosecutor's Office was established as the authorised body for the return of illegally acquired assets. The Chairman of the Committee was appointed by Presidential Decree, dated 21 October 2023.

Once the assets of unexplained origin have been identified, the person concerned may be included in the above-mentioned special Register by decision of the Commission. After that, the assets may be voluntarily returned by the person to the state, or they may be forcibly returned to the state in civil proceedings. When the authorised asset recovery authority has reasonable suspicion about the legality of the sources of acquisition (origin) of the assets of an individual included in the Register, after reviewing the materials by the commission, the prosecutor, based on consideration of all necessary circumstances the recommendations of the commission, may decide to file a lawsuit with the court to return such assets to the state as assets of unexplained origin (Part 1 of Article 27 (2023[10])).

Additionally, it appears that the Law establishes an excessively high threshold for its application. The issue of including a subject and/or its affiliates in the Register shall be submitted to the commission for consideration only if the authorised asset recovery body has reasonable doubts about the legality of the sources of acquisition of assets. This applies when the aggregate amount of those assets is equal to or exceeds thirteen million times the monthly calculation index, which is approximately EUR 100 million (Part 1 of Article 14 (2023[10])).

The specified threshold for the application of the non-conviction-based confiscation concept appears unjustified and significantly restricts the scope of such confiscation to only the wealthiest individuals. Under the rule of law, it should apply to an indeterminate number of persons who fall within clearly defined and justified criteria of legitimate purpose and public interest. Considering this, it is proposed to significantly lower the threshold for the application of such confiscation, depending on the model chosen (in the case of Model 2 - approximately USD 100 000; in the case of Model 3 - approximately USD 30 000).

In its previous analysis of this confiscation model, the OECD noted (2024[9]) that the introduction of the concept of assets of unexplained origin and their confiscation by shifting the burden of proof to the individual controlling such assets would be welcomed. However, a number of provisions of the Law raise concerns. These relate to decisions to include subjects and their affiliates in the special Register of Subjects and their Affiliates, which are made by a Commission headed by the Prime Minister and comprising members of the Government and other political civil servants. According to the Law, this essentially political body is authorised to review information on assets and other information confirming the legality of the sources of acquisition (origin) of declared assets and to form the Register "taking into account socio-economic risks and other factors". Entry in the Register is a prerequisite for applying to the court for the purpose of compulsory seizure of the relevant assets to the state in civil proceedings. The involvement of such a body in the asset confiscation process contradicts the standards of protection of property rights and creates significant corruption risks.

In addition, previous assessment of the Law (OECD, 2024[9]) identified the following areas for improvement which remained unaddressed:

- The vague definition of assets that may be subject to confiscation (assets owned by an individual who possesses or possessed in the past administrative authoritative resources (connections or influence) in relation to public officials.

- The presence of the concept of "indicators of anomalies in the conditions of entrepreneurial activity."
- The possibility of actual "withdrawal" of a criminal case from the investigation by the investigative authorities through the inclusion of the individual under investigation and their assets (which may be regarded as proceeds from criminal activity) in the Register, followed by subsequent negotiations for the voluntary return of such assets without the requisite procedural guarantees and judicial oversight.
- Unlimited discretion in concluding an agreement on voluntary return of assets, including in determining the list of assets to be returned and the terms of return (for example, "the number of jobs created and the efficiency of the use of the asset" as well as "and other factors characterizing the efficiency and conditions of use of the asset" are considered).
- The unjustifiability of granting de facto immunity from criminal prosecution in cases of voluntary return of negotiated assets based on agreements. According to Article 23 of the Law (2023[10]), in the event of a voluntary return of assets based on agreements and the release of individuals from criminal liability, the information provided by them to the Committee cannot be utilised by the Committee or other authorised state bodies for any purposes, including but not limited to: filing lawsuits and applications in courts; investigating new criminal cases registered after the date of the conclusion of said agreements; investigating criminal cases registered prior to the date of these agreements concerning actions unrelated to the assets that are the subject of the agreements; initiating new proceedings for administrative offenses.
- The questionable role of the declaration of asset disclosure, which is submitted voluntarily.

Considering that confiscation based on the Law of the Republic of Kazakhstan "On the Return of Illegally Acquired Assets to the State" (2023[10]) is not criminal confiscation in its essence, as well as the fact that the practice of its application is not public (court decisions on these categories of cases in the Kazakhstan are withheld from the public, which makes it impossible to study, generalise and prepare recommendations based on the practice of application of this instrument), this study further focuses exclusively on the practice of application of criminal types of confiscation.

Recommendations

- Bring the legal framework for criminal confiscation into full compliance with international standards, in particular, UNCAC (2004[3]) and best practices in the ACN region by ensuring a transition from the existing hybrid model of confiscation as a sanction to that of confiscation of instruments (tools and means) of a crime, proceeds of criminal offenses and any benefit therefrom (as a criminal law measure other than a sanction).
- Ensure that revised framework for confiscation of instruments, proceeds and benefits of criminal offenses applies to all corruption-related criminal offenses without exception (including corruption in the private sector).
- Make a clear distinction between the objects of the updated confiscation model and the concept of material evidence to eliminate overlaps and challenges with law enforcement in practice (ensuring that the confiscation of instruments, proceeds and benefits of corruption and other proceeds-generating crimes that have material value are prioritised).
- Before the implementation of the above recommended reform of the framework for criminal confiscation, as an interim measure, exclude all corruption offenses from the scope of application of Part 4 of Article 55 of the CC (2014[5]) by supplementing the list of relevant offenses in Part 8 of Article 55 of the CC.

3 Confiscation for high-level corruption

This chapter looks into the numerical data of confiscation in corruption cases, including the value of confiscated assets and portion of court judgments imposing confiscation. The chapter also analyses the relation between the type of corruption offense and frequency of the confiscation being imposed. Additionally, the chapter assesses the practice of application of confiscation measures in high-level corruption cases.

For the purpose of analysing the status of criminal confiscation in corruption cases, this study only considers offenses related to corruption as defined by UNCAC (2004[3]), rather than according to the definitions used in statistical reports adopted in Kazakhstan. Accordingly, corruption offenses for this study include acts stipulated by the following provisions of the CC (2014[5]):

- misappropriation or embezzlement of entrusted property (Para 2, Part 3, article 189 of the CC (2014[5]))
- legalisation (laundering) of money and (or) other property obtained by criminal means (Para 1, part 3, article 218 of the CC)
- abuse of official powers (Article 361 of the CC)
- taking a bribe (Article 366 of the CC)
- bribery (Article 367 of the CC)
- mediation in bribery (Article 368 of the CC (2014[5]))[3].

According to the official criminal pre-trial statistics for 2021–2023, provided for the purposes of this study, various assets of the following value and in the following amounts were seized during the pre-trial investigation stage for the listed six categories of crimes:

- Kazakhstani tenge (KZT) 411 349 600 (approximately USD 794 509) in 2021,
- KZT 7 434 468 800 (approximately USD 14 359 442) in 2022, and
- KZT 6 240 858 400 (approximately USD 12 054 021) in 2023.

3.1 Statistics on seized and confiscated assets

According to the statistics, from 2021 to 2023, property seizure was not applied at all in cases of money laundering and bribery intermediation. Additionally, the amounts of seized assets in criminal cases represented a minimal percentage of the "established value of material harm" from the relevant crimes in 2021 (4.7%), rising to 62.7% in 2022, but dropping to 13.3% in 2023.

However, even with these figures, it is challenging to clearly discern trends in this area, as the statistics include a column for an aggregate figure of "seized and voluntarily repaid" assets at the investigation stage. For certain types of crimes, such as abuse of office, these "voluntary returns" constitute a significant portion of the total. It is important to note that the statistics are compiled in a way that prevents the separation of seized assets from voluntarily repaid amounts, as these indicators are aggregated into a single figure.

The study analysed 48 verdicts from first-level courts across various regions of Kazakhstan, issued in cases involving corruption-related income-generating crimes during the period from 2021 to 2023. The analysis of these verdicts revealed that property seizure was not imposed in every corruption case; for instance, 25 out of the 48 verdicts (more than a half) did not mention property seizure in the corresponding criminal proceedings at all.

In most cases, seizure is imposed on the object of the bribe, either seized during the apprehension of the individual caught in the act or voluntarily handed over during such an apprehension (the total amounts of seized objects of bribes are generally insignificant). The minor size of the seized bribe amounts is also confirmed by the overall official statistics: in 2021, property worth KZT 91 302 900 (approximately USD 176 349) was seized in bribery cases; in 2022, KZT 49 000 000 (approximately USD 94 642) and in 2023, KZT 56 077 200 (approximately USD 108 311).

Other assets, seized during investigation stage, are often released by the court upon the issuance of a verdict on the grounds that the criminal origin of the seized property has not been proven, in accordance with the requirements of Article 48 of the CC (2014[5]). The available statistics do not allow for a reliable determination of the type of property that was seized whether it was an instrument (tool or means of committing a corrupt crime), proceeds from a corrupt crime, or any other benefit derived from it; whether the seized property belonged to the suspect, the accused, or a third party (individual or legal entity); and so on.

According to the official court statistics provided for the purposes of this study, from 2021 to 2023, confiscation was applied in 57 cases pertaining to criminal cases of corruption. In 2021, there were 15 such verdicts (including 4 for misappropriation, 2 for abuse of authority, 5 for passive bribery and 4 for giving bribes); in 2022, there were 12 (including 1 for misappropriation, 10 for passive bribery and 1 for bribery intermediation); and in 2023, there were 30 (including 5 for misappropriation, 4 for money laundering, 1 for abuse of authority, 14 for passive bribery and 6 for giving bribes).

Table 3.1. Number of corruption cases with a confiscation order

Type of crime	2021	2022	2023	Number of cases
Embezzlement or misappropriation (Article 189 Part.3 Para 2, Article 189 Part 4 of CC)	4	1	5	10
Money laundering (Article 218 Part 3 Para 1 of CC)	-	-	4	4
Abuse of official powers (Article 361 of CC)	2	-	1	3
Receiving a bribe (Article 366 of CC)	5	10	14	29
Giving a bribery (Article 367 of CC)	4	-	6	10
Mediation in bribery (Article 368 of CC)	-	1	-	1
Total	**15**	**12**	**30**	**57**

Source: Official judicial statistics for 2021–2023 provided by the authorities

It should be noted that the judicial statistics on the number of confiscation orders in corruption cases for 2023, provided for the purposes of this study (30 cases), differ from 25 cases reported by the country for the purposes of the baseline monitoring of the fifth round (OECD, 2024[9]) under IAP. This discrepancy suggests potential challenges related to the collection and processing of statistical data.

The current approach to recording confiscation orders and decisions presents obstacles to drawing reliable conclusions about the use of this tool in corruption cases based on the available statistics. However, there is an opportunity for further improvement in the methods of analysis and assessment.

Nonetheless, the available data indicate that criminal confiscation in cases involving income-generating corruption offenses is not consistently applied, highlighting the potential for enhancing its effectiveness.

The number of confiscations compared to the total number of revenue-generating corruption offenses appears insignificant. According to official pre-trial and judicial statistics, 2728 criminal cases involving potentially revenue-generating corruption offenses were brought to court between 2021 and 2023 (899 cases in 2021, 868 cases in 2022 and 961 cases in 2023). The 57 corruption cases in which confiscation was imposed by the courts during this period represent only 2.09%.

Official judicial statistics do not provide information on the amount or value of assets for which courts have issued criminal confiscation orders. However, the Anti-Corruption Agency[4] has collected its own statistics regarding the value of assets confiscated through court orders, contributing to a more complete analysis, though it does not fully account for aspects of actual implementation:

In 2021, the courts ordered confiscation of a total of KZT 429 436 257 (approximately USD 829 443) in embezzlement cases, KZT 2 330 000 (approximately USD 4 500) in bribery cases, and KZT 10 000 (approximately USD 19) in bribery cases.

In 2022, the total confiscation was amounted to KZT 1 565 377 226 (approximately USD 3 023 477) in one embezzlement case, KZT 15 931 062 (approximately USD 30 770) in bribery cases, and KZT 50 000 (approximately USD 97) in a bribery mediation case.

In 2023, the total confiscated amounts were KZT 25 239 485 714 (approximately USD 48 749 269) in embezzlement cases, KZT 904 213 180 (approximately USD 1 746 459) in money laundering cases, KZT 163 755 667 (approximately USD 316 289) in abuse of office cases, KZT 7 259 940 (approximately USD 14 022) in passive bribery cases, and KZT 13 432 598 (approximately USD 25 945) in active bribery cases.

Table 3.2. Increase in the value of confiscated assets under court decisions

Value of assets confiscated by court decisions (USD) *

Type of crime	2021	2022	2023	Total
Embezzlement or misappropriation (Article 189 Part.3 Para 2, Article 189 Part 4 of the CC)	829 443	3 023 477	48 749 269	52 602 189
Receiving a bribe (Article 366 of the CC)	4 500	30 770	14 022	49 292
Giving a bribe (Article 367 of the CC)	-	-	25 945	26 945
Mediation in bribery (Article 368 of the CC)	19	97	-	16
Money laundering (Article 218 Part 3 Para 1 of the CC)	-	-	1 746 459	1 746 459
Abuse of office (Article 361 of the CC)	-	-	316 289	316 289
Total	**833 962**	**3 054 344**	**50 851 984**	**54 740 290**

Note: * Approximate equivalents in USD
Source: Data provided by the Anti-Corruption Agency of the Republic of Kazakhstan.

The statistics presented suggests that most of the property is seized and confiscated in embezzlement cases (Para 2 of Part 3 of Article 189 of the CC (2014[5])), while seizure and confiscation of property for passive and active bribery offenses remain insignificant over years. Considering the scale of the country and the economy, such figures of criminal confiscation in corruption cases do not appear convincing.

These findings are consistent with the conclusions of the OECD analysis (OECD, 2017[8]) that covered a period from 2014 to 2016. The monitoring noted that the analysis of the statistics demonstrated that the amount of seized and confiscated property for the main corruption offenses was decreasing. That was particularly evident in confiscations in passive bribery cases: EUR 7 600 000 in 2014, EUR 1 100 000 in 2015 and only EUR 481 000 in 2016. At the same time, most of the seized and confiscated property was related to such offenses as embezzlement and misappropriation of entrusted property, as well as abuse of office. In general, it can be noted that the volumes of seized (confiscated) property are relatively small, considering the size of Kazakhstan's economy.

Above figures indicate that the situation has remained virtually unchanged from 2021 to 2023, with the amounts of confiscations in bribery cases showing a further decline since 2014–2016.

Overall, the relatively small amounts of seized and confiscated property are notable, especially considering the size of Kazakhstan's economy. As highlighted in the analysis, there has been little change during this period, and the amounts of confiscations in bribery cases have decreased further.

A significant indicator for assessing the effectiveness of the confiscation system is the amount of property actually confiscated and the percentage ratio of this amount to the value of assets specified in court confiscation orders. In response to inquiries regarding the funds received by the state budget as a result of enforcing relevant court decisions on corruption offenses from 2021 to 2023, authorities reported that KZT 58 504 305 (approximately USD 113 000) was credited to the budget in 2021, KZT 211 621 513 (approximately USD 408 740) and USD 14 700 in 2022 and KZT 22 687 305 587 (approximately

USD 43 819 814) and USD 50 700 in 2023. Notably, KZT 19 600 000 000 of this amount was the value of a waste disposal plant that was confiscated in one case.

Table 3.3. Increase in the effectiveness of confiscation measures in corruption cases

Value of assets recovered based on confiscation orders (USD)*

	2021	2022	2023	Total
Amount of actually confiscated actives	113 000	423 440	43 870 514	44 406 954
Amount of confiscated assets under court decisions	833 962	3 054 344	50 851 984	54 740 290
Percentage ratio	**13.5**	**13.9**	**86.3**	**81.1**

Note: *Approximate equivalents in USD
Source: Data provided by the Anti-Corruption Agency of the Republic of Kazakhstan

3.2 Confiscation in high-level corruption cases

The legislation of Kazakhstan does not define the concepts of high-level corruption or high-ranking corruption, nor does it establish criteria for categorizing such cases.

For the purposes of this study, the term "high-level corruption" shall be understood in accordance with the definition provided in the Istanbul Anti-Corruption Action Plan, 5th Round of Monitoring: Guide (OECD, 2023[12]).

Concept of high-level corruption

"High-level corruption": corruption offences are offenses which meet one of the following criteria:

A. Involve high-level officials in any capacity punishable by criminal law (for example, as masterminds, perpetrators, abettors, or accessories).
B. Involve substantial benefits for officials, their family members, or other related persons (for example, legal persons they own or control, political parties they belong to).

A substantial benefit means a pecuniary benefit that is equal to or exceeds the amount of 1 000 monthly statutory minimum wages (or the equivalent of the minimum wage if it is not applicable) fixed in the respective country on 1 January of the year for which data is provided.

"High-level officials": The following appointed or elected officials:

A. The President, members of Parliament, members of Government and their deputies.
B. Heads of central executive bodies and other central public authorities and their deputies, members of collegiate central public authorities, including independent market regulators and supervisory authorities.
C. Head and members of the board of the national bank, supreme audit institution.
D. Judges of general courts and the constitutional court, prosecutors, members of the highest judicial or prosecutorial governance bodies (for example, a judicial or prosecutorial council).
E. Regional governors or heads of regional administrations, capital city mayor.
F. Ambassadors and heads of diplomatic missions.
G. Any other public officials explicitly designated as politically exposed persons by the national anti-money laundering legislation.

Source: Istanbul Anti-Corruption Action Plan, 5th Round of Monitoring: Guide (OECD, 2023[12])

Out of 48 cases reviewed, only 5 of them qualified as high-level corruption cases: 4 were categorised based on the position held (Head of a central state body, sentenced on 1 February 2021; a Vice-Minister, sentenced on 27 October 2023; Head of the Collegium of the Regional Court, sentenced on 23 November 2023; a judge of a City Court, sentenced on 1 December 2023; and one case qualified based on the criterion of substantial benefit (General Director of a limited liability partnership (LLP), imputed damage from embezzlement of approximately USD 30 000 000, sentenced on 15 September 2023).

Box 3.1. Case of the head of a central state body

The head of a central state body, A, was convicted for conspiracy to commit embezzlement. The court determined that the total amount embezzled was KZT 6 527 956 994 (approximately USD 12 608 542), leading to the conviction of a total of 21 defendants in the case.

In its verdict, the court noted that A was not found to possess any property obtained by criminal means or acquired with funds derived from criminal activity. Therefore, property confiscation as an additional penalty was not imposed. The court also ordered all defendants to jointly and severally compensate the sum of KZT 6 503 045 293 for the damages incurred. To ensure the reparation of damages and meeting the civil claim in the case, the court upheld the prior seizure of the defendants' property, including a 1999 Daewoo Nexia car owned by A.

Source: Court verdict in case No. 7511-20-00-1/223, dated 1 February 2021.

This approach to the confiscation of corruption benefits from a high-ranking official, convicted of an income-generating corruption offense, can hardly be deemed effective or deterrent for both the convicted individual and other public officials. It appears that the income derived from corruption by the official, Y, has not been established, and their relevant assets that could be subject to confiscation were not identified or seized during the investigation (except for Nexia car). Consequently, no confiscation was imposed.

Moreover, the approach in which 21 convicted individuals, including the high-ranking official, are held jointly and severally liable for compensation of damages under a civil suit with a common claim, applying equally to all convicted persons, does not support the principle that crime should not pay. Under such conditions for compensation of the damages incurred, the official has the opportunity to avoid bearing actual financial costs, at least in proportion to their role in the commission of the crime. The value of damages may be recovered from other convicted individuals or not recovered in part or in full.

Box 3.2. Case of a Vice-Minister for Investment and Development

The Vice-Minister of Kazakhstan for Investment and Development, Y, was convicted for abuse of office. The court determined that Y, by concluding the subsoil use contract for mining with a company affiliated with him, illegally transferred for extraction a nickel-cobalt deposit. As a result of the criminal offense, the state suffered significant losses as not accrued profits amounting to KZT 40 638 265 000 (approximately USD 78 491 525).

The court noted that no civil claim had been filed in the criminal case and that the territory of the deposit had been returned to the state through a judicial process. The verdict lacks any argumentation regarding the calculation of the benefit received by the defendant from the commission of the corruption crime. However, the court found that some property belonging to the defendant were acquired during or after the commission of the incriminated offense. The court was of the opinion that these assets were "accordingly acquired with funds obtained by criminal means," and thus deemed it necessary to confiscate them for the state. The confiscated assets included various shares in 13 companies, real estate (two land plots, a garden house, and a summer house with land), two luxury cars – a 2021 Mercedes-Benz Maybach S580 and a 2021 Bentley Bentayga V8, and Y's funds in bank accounts in insignificant amounts, as well as five gold bars weighing a total of 70 grams. The court lifted the seizure of apartment belonging to Y, justifying this by stating that it was a service apartment that had been privatised in accordance with the law.

Source: Court verdict in the case No. 7135-23-00-1/338, dated 27 October 2023.

The acquisition of property during or after the commission of a crime can serve as indirect evidence of its illicit origin. However, the mere fact of acquisition within a certain timeframe, without additional supporting evidence, may not be sufficient to establish, beyond a reasonable doubt, the asset's connection to a specific crime.

The following case example demonstrates the practice of not imposing confiscation in the circumstances when a bribe item has been recovered.

Box 3.3. Case of the Chairman of the Judicial Collegium of the Regional Court

The Chairman of the Judicial Panel for Administrative Cases of a Regional Court, M, was convicted of taking a bribe through extortion in the amount of KZT 19 000 000 (approximately USD 38 000) in exchange for issuing an agreed ruling on an administrative case. The court noted that no property obtained through criminal means was established to belong to the defendant, M, and deemed it appropriate not to impose the confiscation as an additional penalty due to the absence of the relevant property. Furthermore, since the tool of the offense, cash in the amount of KZT 19 000 000, was submitted by the victim (a bribe-giver) to the investigative authority during the crime scene examination, the court ordered its return to the victim, i.e., the bribe-giver.

Source: Court verdict in the case No. 3911-23-00-1/254, dated 23 November 2023.

In the following example, the justification for the application of confiscation appears questionable because the only criteria used by the court was the fact of acquisition of the confiscated property after commission of the offenses.

Box 3.4. Case on embezzlement in the private sector

The court accepted a plea agreement for the managers of three private companies, who were charged with conspiracy to commit embezzlement and money laundering. The total value of embezzled assets was KZT 14 565 318 010 (approximately USD 28 132 451). The damage was voluntarily reimbursed by the defendants in full at the investigation stage. In considering the imposition of confiscation, the court referred to Article 48 of the CC (2014[5]) and removed seizure from all property of the defendants acquired by them before committing the offenses. Court noted that "it is not property obtained by criminal means". And since two defendants were found to have property that was acquired after the commission of the offenses, all the said property was confiscated by the court as "obtained by criminal means and acquired with funds obtained by criminal means" (residential and commercial premises, a land plot, funds in bank accounts). The total value of these assets surpassed KZT 3 000 000 000 and approximately USD 7 850 000. Thus, the court applied the approach that everything acquired by the defendants after the commission of the crime is automatically considered "criminally obtained or acquired with funds obtained by criminal means".

Source: Court verdict in the case No. 7199-23-00-1a/210, dated 15 November 2023.

It might be possible to presume the criminal origin of assets (even those acquired before the charged offense) if Kazakhstan had a legal framework for extended confiscation. However, such a framework would necessitate clear criteria for recognizing property as subject to confiscation. Mere acquisition of the property after the commission of an offense would not be sufficient. The law should also provide guarantees of a fair trial for the property owner.

The following example illustrates the practice of courts in Kazakhstan, which typically do not consider bribe amounts as criminally obtained property and, consequently, do not apply confiscation on that basis. However, the bribe amount is directed to state income under different legal grounds.

Box 3.5. Case against a city court judge

A judge from a city court was convicted of taking a bribe of KZT 2 000 000 (approximately USD 3 860) in exchange for imposing a non-custodial sentence in a criminal case. In considering the application of confiscation, the court referenced Article 48 of the CC (2014[5]), noting that the defendant did not possess any property obtained by criminal means, nor any property acquired with funds derived from criminal activity, or property that served as a tool or means of committing the crime. Consequently, the court did not impose confiscation as an additional penalty.

The bribe of KZT 2 000 000 was seized during the arrest and searches of the defendant's car and home. The court ordered that the bribe amount of KZT 2 000 000 be converted to the income of the state as "material evidence".

Source: Court verdict in the case No. 3140-23-00-1/76, dated 1 December 2023.

The five high-level corruption convictions described above highlight the gaps in the existing criminal confiscation regime in Kazakhstan and generally support the conclusion that it requires further improvement.

Considering the data on the practical application of seizure and confiscation measures in corruption cases, including those involving high-level corruption, it is necessary, following the recommended reforms to the confiscation institution, to implement comprehensive measures aimed at strengthening the capacity of investigators and prosecutors involved in prosecuting corruption cases, as well as judges who preside over these types of cases.

The Baseline Report of the Fifth Round of Monitoring of Anti-Corruption Reforms in Kazakhstan under the IAP (OECD, 2024[9]) provides insights from non-governmental stakeholders regarding the current regime for confiscating corrupt assets. In particular, they have noted the following issues:

- Measures to confiscate illegally obtained property in Kazakhstan are applied very ineffectively, despite the existence of an appropriate legislative framework. Article 15 of CPC (2014[6]) states that confiscation may occur before a sentence is issued, but in practice, this tool is rarely utilised.
- Courts primarily focus on ordering the confiscation of the object of the bribe and compensation for damages in cases involving embezzlement or malfeasance. Even when case files contain documented evidence of property transferred to an official as remuneration, the confiscation process is seldom executed. In the best scenarios, only the seizure of property is maintained until the damage is fully compensated.
- In bribery cases with multiple episodes, investigative authorities often fail to identify or evaluate the property acquired through illegal means, leading to courts not ordering confiscation. Similarly, in embezzlement cases, investigations typically do not ascertain how the stolen money was used. If proceeds from crime were utilised to generate more property, indirect proceeds are also excluded from confiscation.

Moreover, courts do not proactively initiate the confiscation of property involved in corruption offenses. Instances of confiscation targeting the property of high-ranking officials remain isolated, highlighting significant shortcomings in the confiscation system and the urgent need for reform.

According to non-governmental stakeholders, the current regime of criminal confiscation in Kazakhstan is ineffective, echoing arguments similar to those identified in the Baseline Report of the 5th round of monitoring for Kazakhstan (OECD, 2024[9]).

Non-governmental organisations stress the importance of transparency in the voluntary asset recovery process. They argue that what is referred to in the country as voluntary asset recovery may reflect aspects of non-conviction-based confiscation of illegally obtained property. A special committee has been established within the Prosecutor General`s Office, marking a step towards a more organised approach to forced asset recovery. However, it is crucial to ensure that the activities of this committee are transparent and accessible to the public.

Additionally, activities and decisions of an asset recovery commission are not publicly accessible. Information regarding the register of entities whose assets are subject to recovery is also unavailable to the public. As a result, both the public and the media lack access to data concerning the processes of tracing or seizing the proceeds of corruption and funds used to commit crimes.

In relation to high-level corruption, non-governmental organisations highlight certain mechanisms that allow individuals to evade accountability for corrupt acts and retain their assets. These mechanisms include plea bargaining, the voluntary return of illegally acquired assets to the state, and the absence of effective confiscation measures. Non-governmental organisations (NGO) further emphasise that accountability for corruption offenses is often influenced by political or temporary considerations.

The OECD has noted (2024[9]) that several criminal trials involving relatives of the former President were recorded in 2023. While these cases may raise questions about potential political motivations, the sentences imposed have been varied. For instance, one influential relative convicted of embezzling KZT 14 billion from a state-owned company, received a prison sentence in September 2023 but was released on 6 November 2023, following the return of illegally acquired assets and the replacement of the unexecuted portion of the sentence with a suspended one. However, journalistic investigations revealed that the actual return of assets did not occur (2025[13]), indicating opportunities for further improvement and development of the law enforcement system.

During interviews conducted for this study, investigators and prosecutors noted that establishing material harm is essential to proving the elements of corruption offenses. Although this requirement is not explicitly stated in the law, it reflects prevailing practice. In some cases, establishing such harm necessitates conducting an audit or economic forensic expertise. They also pointed out that the concept of illicit gains from corruption (i.e., corruption proceeds) is not applied in practice, largely due to legal traditions that have persisted since the Soviet era. Furthermore, they indicated that the application of certain confiscation mechanisms, such as confiscation of property transferred to third parties, value-based confiscation and confiscation before conviction, poses practical challenges.

The existing system for statistical reporting on property confiscation, including cases of high-level corruption, requires further improvement. Notably, data on high-level corruption cases is absent from the statistics, as current legislation lacks definitions or criteria for such cases, and no statistics are maintained in this regard. The statistical data—along with practice—primarily reflect so-called voluntary returns, which do not constitute confiscation in an international legal sense as defined in Article 31 of the UNCAC (United Nations, 2004[3]).

Existing statistical reports fail to differentiate between types of confiscations (criminal confiscation under Article 48 of the CC (2014[5]); confiscation of evidence under Article 118 of CPC; confiscation without conviction pursuant to Section 15, Chapter 71 of CPC (2014[6])) or between the subjects of confiscation measures (including instruments (tools and means), proceeds of crime (both direct and indirect), profits, other benefits, mixed proceeds, equivalent confiscation, and confiscation from third parties (individuals and legal entities)).

Confiscations conducted in absentia and based on various types of procedural agreements are also not separately identified. Additionally, there is a lack of data regarding the amounts and values of assets subject to court decisions on confiscation and the sums received in the budget as a result of enforcing such confiscation orders. The list of corruption offenses in statistical reports extends well beyond the internationally recognised definition of corruption offenses, distorting the statistics and excluding offenses in the private sector, among others.

A properly configured statistics system for confiscation measures would enable an accurate assessment of the current situation regarding criminal confiscation in practice, identification of trends, formulation of precise conclusions, and planning of measures to improve the existing confiscation system, particularly in corruption cases.

Considering the data collected on the practical application of property seizure and confiscation measures in criminal proceedings related to corruption—including high-level corruption—it seems necessary, following the recommended reforms to the institution of confiscation, to adopt comprehensive measures aimed at strengthening the capacity of investigators and prosecutors handling corruption cases, as well as judges presiding over these categories of cases. It may also be advisable to consider introducing specialization for investigators and prosecutors involved in the criminal prosecution of corruption, particularly high-level corruption, focusing exclusively on financial investigations, asset detection, and recovery.

Additionally, it would be advisable to improve the approach to criminal confiscation statistics so that all the indicators described above are reflected in the new reporting forms where possible and that the updated statistics are made publicly available to ensure that they are transparent and accessible to the public.

Recommendations

- Make it a priority for investigators and prosecutors to fully pursue the confiscation of proceeds of corruption (or their equivalents), particularly in cases of high-level corruption.
- Consider introducing a specialisation for investigators and prosecutors focused exclusively on financial investigations, asset detection, and recovery in corruption cases, particularly of high-level corruption.
- Implement measures to ensure that property seizure and confiscation are systematically and consistently applied in practice in cases of corruption offenses involving illicit income.
- Improve keeping the statistics on criminal confiscations by including detailed data that distinguishes between types of criminal confiscations and objects of confiscation measures, including confiscation from third parties (natural and legal persons). This should include differentiating between the types and levels of officials subject to confiscation measures, as well as the types of corrupt benefits obtained and confiscated. Additionally, include data on the amounts or value of assets subject to court confiscation orders and the total funds received by the budget as a result of these confiscations.
- Ensure that detailed statistics on criminal confiscation in corruption cases, including high-level corruption, are published periodically (at least annually) to guarantee transparency and accessibility for the public.

4 Application of different types of confiscation

The chapter looks into the practice of application of different types of confiscation for corruption offenses based on available case-law, interviews with practitioners and the open sources. The chapter specifically spotlight identified deficiencies in the relevant judicial practice and recommends venues for improvement.

4.1 Confiscation of instruments of corruption offenses

In accordance with the UNCAC (United Nations, 2004[3]), each State Party is required to adopt, to the fullest extent possible within its domestic legal system, measures necessary to enable the confiscation of property, equipment, and other instruments used or intended for use in committing offenses recognised under this Convention (Article 31(1)(b)). This provision pertains to the confiscation of so-called instruments of crime – means and tools employed in committing corruption, which are objects that facilitate or simplify the commission of an offense.

The law mandates the confiscation of property that is used as an instrument or means of committing a criminal offense (Para 4 of Part 2 of Article 48 of the CC (2014[5])). Meanwhile, under Para 1 pf Part 1 of Article 118 of CPC (2014[6]), objects that have served as instruments or means of committing a criminal offense must be recognised as material evidence. However, both the CC and CPC lack definitions for what constitutes instruments and means of committing a crime.

An analysis of five guilty verdicts from the courts of Kazakhstan regarding high-level corruption cases from 2021 to 2023 revealed that none of these cases involved the confiscation of instruments used to commit such offenses. Additionally, an examination of the remaining 43 out of 48 analysed verdicts indicated that none referenced the confiscation of corruption offense instruments. While confiscation of the object of bribery in an active bribery scenario could be considered a form of confiscation, only three of the 48 verdicts pertained to the prosecution of individuals for active bribery under Article 367 of the CC (2014[5]), and none held the bribe recipient accountable. Out of these three cases, the court actually applied confiscation of the "object of the bribe" as "material evidence" in only one case, although it used the term "convert to state revenue" rather than "confiscate" (Case No. 3911–21-00-1/297). In the other two verdicts within this category, the object of the bribe was not confiscated (Case No. 1–336/2021, Case No. 7525-21-00-1/281), and both court rulings were silent on this issue.

The Baseline Report of the Fifth Round of Monitoring of Anti-Corruption Reforms in Kazakhstan (OECD, 2024[9]) cites two examples from 2023. In one case, upon the conviction of individuals for active bribery, mobile phones, SIM cards, and flash drives were confiscated for state revenue. In the second case, mobile phones were confiscated on the grounds they were used to commit the offense. Bribes were also confiscated.

Thus, from the reviewed judicial practice, it can be concluded that there have been no cases of confiscation of instruments of crime in high-level corruption cases, and in cases of other corruption offenses only a case of "conversion by the court to the income of the state of the object of a bribe" as "material evidence" in case of active bribery[5] and two cases of conversion to the income of the state of the object of a bribe and cell phones, SIM cards and flash cards used in the commission of active bribery were found.

At the same time, as practice shows, the courts often do not refer to Para 4 Part 2 of Article 48 of the CC (2014[5]), which allows for the confiscation of property that is a tool or means of committing a crime. Instead, they apply Article 118 of CPC (2014[6]), which regulates issues related to decision-making on material evidence. According to Para 1 of Part 1 of Article 118 of CPC, objects are recognised as material evidence if there is reason to believe they served as instruments or means of committing a crime. In the studied court practices, there are instances where the decision regarding the fate of the object of a bribe in cases of active bribery is not made at all, with no explanation provided, meaning that confiscation of such a bribe in any form is not executed.

The reliance on the concept of material evidence and its conversion to state revenue instead of outright confiscation of instruments of crime, along with the failure to apply confiscation to the object of a bribe in cases of active bribery, is inconsistent with the approaches outlined in the UNCAC (United Nations,

2004[3]). This undermines the critical message that property, enabling and facilitating the commission of corruption offenses, is subject to unconditional confiscation.

One significant reason for this situation is the current model of criminal confiscation in Kazakhstan, which, as previously recommended, should be aligned with international standards. This means that instruments (means and tools) of crime must be clearly defined in the law or, at a minimum, established through consistent judicial practice, thus making them mandatory subjects of confiscation measures. Additionally, the duality of regulation, which currently mixes instruments as objects of confiscation with material evidence, should be addressed.

4.2 Confiscation of proceeds of crime

The UNCAC (United Nations, 2004[3]) obliges each State Party to adopt, to the fullest extent possible within its domestic legal system, measures that may be necessary to enable the confiscation of proceeds from offenses recognised as such under this Convention, or property the value of which corresponds to the value of such proceeds (Article 31(1)(a)). According to Article 2(e) of the Convention (United Nations, 2004[3]), "proceeds of crime" means any property acquired or obtained, directly or indirectly, as a result of the commission of any offense.

If the proceeds of crime have been transformed or converted, in whole or in part, into other property, confiscation measures apply to such property (Article 31(4) (United Nations, 2004[3])). If such proceeds of crime have been commingled with property acquired from lawful sources, confiscation applies to that portion of the property that corresponds to the assessed value of the commingled proceeds (Article 31(5)). Measures outlined in Article 31 of the Convention also apply to profits or other benefits derived from such proceeds of crime, from property into which such proceeds have been transformed or converted, or from property to which such proceeds of crime have been commingled, in the same manner and to the same extent as they apply to the proceeds of crime (Article 31(6)).

Judicial practice in corruption cases from 2021 to 2023 reveals that, in most cases involving criminal proceedings for corruption, the courts nevertheless consider, in one way or another, the issue of criminal confiscation or its equivalents within the legal framework of Kazakhstan.

In this context, three main types of verdicts can be identified:

- In bribery cases, verdicts often involve returning the object of the bribe as material evidence to the state or recovering the value of the undiscovered object of the bribe from the defendant for the state. The vast majority of the verdicts studied fall under this category.
- In cases of theft6 and abuse of office, court verdicts often involve the confiscation of property owned by the convicted individual that was obtained through criminal means or purchased with proceeds from criminal activities, as an additional penalty under Part 1 of Article 48 of the CC (2014[5]). For example, in three high-level corruption cases (No. 7135-23-00-1/338, No. 7199-23-00-1a/210 and No. 7511-20-00-1/223), the property was recognised as obtained through criminal means or purchased with criminal proceeds based solely on the temporal sequence - the acquisition of the property occurred after the commission of the offense. Two additional examples, following the same approach in criminal cases of theft, are detailed in the Baseline Report of the Fifth Round of Monitoring of Anti-Corruption Reforms in Kazakhstan (OECD, 2024[9]). In such cases, a civil claim may also be satisfied, or "damages" may be fully compensated at the investigation stage under "voluntary return".
- In cases of theft and abuse of office, court verdicts regarding compensation for damages caused by corruption offenses are often made through the satisfaction of a civil claim within the criminal case or directly from the seized assets of the defendants. For instance, in case No. 7511-20-00-1/223, the court ruled to jointly recover damages from all 21 defendants.

The judicial practices from 2021 to 2023 indicate that the provisions of Para 1 Part 2, Article 48 of the CC, which mandate the confiscation of money and other property obtained as a result of the crime, as well as any income derived from them, are virtually not applied by the courts to corruption revenues. Specifically, in cases of passive bribery, bribes are primarily treated by the courts as "tools of the crime" and "material evidence" under Article 118 of CPC (2014[6]). In such instances, the courts often lift the seizure from previously arrested property of the defendants, citing the absence of established criminal origin for the property, i.e., that it was obtained through criminal means or purchased with proceeds derived from criminal activities, as required by Part 1 of Article 48 of the CC (2014[5]) (cases No. 7150–22-00-1/91 and No. 7141-23-00-1/852).

Following is a typical formulation found in the studied verdicts for criminal cases of bribery, particularly passive bribery: "There are no grounds for imposing an additional penalty in the form of confiscation of property, as provided by the sanction of the article, and for the application of Article 48 of the CC (2014[5]), since the investigative body did not establish property obtained through criminal means and therefore subject to confiscation, in accordance with the requirements of Article 48 of the CC."

The accepted bribe is not considered by the courts as proceeds from crime. The dispositive part of the verdict states that material evidence, funds in the amount of [specified amount] tenge, stored in the custody of the Anti-Corruption Service, shall be confiscated for state revenue (verdict of 25 April 2022, case No. 7525–22-00-1/97). This approach diverges from the generally accepted international standard regarding confiscation the proceeds of corruption offenses, as well as any profits or other benefits derived therefrom.

Moreover, some verdicts revealed that, in principle, a court did not decide on the merits of the criminal proceeds, such as the confiscation of the bribe itself in passive bribery (even as "material evidence") or its equivalent value (e.g., cases No. 3140-20-00-1/108, No. 910-21-21-00-1/257, No. 3111-21-21-00-1/375 and others).The use of the concept of material evidence and its conversion into state revenue instead of confiscation of criminal proceeds, as well as the non-application of confiscation to the object of the bribe (proceeds of corruption in case of passive bribery), is not in line with the approach of the UNCAC and does not transmit the necessary message that any property acquired or obtained, directly or indirectly, as a result of the commission of a corruption offense, as well as any profit or other benefits therefrom, is subject to unconditional confiscation in such cases.

In cases of other corruption offenses, such as embezzlement and abuse of office, the judicial practice in Kazakhstan applies the concept of “damage” from the crime rather than “benefit from corruption offense”. In these cases, courts typically confiscate only the property acquired after or during the commission of the crime solely on this basis, and recognising such property as meeting the requirements of Part 1 of Article 48 of the CC (2014[5]). For instance, in one case, the property of two convicted individuals was confiscated under Part 1 of Article 48 of the CC due to its acquisition after the crime, despite the verdict confirming that the entire incriminated 'damage' from theft was fully compensated by the defendants before the verdict was issued (Case No. 7199-23-00-1a/210).

In some cases, the court allows property to remain under further seizure to ensure the enforcement of a civil claim regarding compensation for damages caused by the crime (e.g., case No. 7511–20-00-1/223). However, such property was of a symbolic nature. In the aforementioned case, only a 1999 Daewoo Nexia vehicle was seized, while the total amount of damages to be jointly compensated was KZT 6 503 045 293.

A typical example of the judicial approach can be seen in the court’s verdict in case No. 7511–20-00-1/223. The court established that during the commission of the offense, the defendant acquired property using funds generated through criminal means, making it subject to confiscation for state revenue. Specifically, the defendant acquired two cars. However, no further justification was provided to establish a link between these assets and the income from the alleged crime, apart from their purchase occurring during the ongoing criminal activity.

It should be noted that the international concept of confiscation of proceeds of crime, as stated in Article 31(1)(a) of the UNCAC (United Nations, 2004[3]), requires the existence and proof of a link between the property (either direct or indirect, through conversion or transformation) and the corresponding income-generating offense. The mere acquisition of property after or during the commission of a crime does not automatically establish such a connection.

For assets without a proven link to a specific crime, an alternative regime for confiscation exists, such as expanded confiscation in criminal proceedings or other procedures. Therefore, the legal concept and application of criminal confiscation to proceeds of crime in Kazakhstan should be aligned with international standards in this regard. Notably, only one verdict out of the 48 involved the confiscation of proceeds from a specific corruption offense (embezzlement).

Box 4.1. Confiscation of proceeds from a specific corruption offense

The defendant, A, had a 2012 Mercedes-Benz SL 500 confiscated by court order as one of the proceeds of embezzlement, they were convicted of. The court explained in its ruling that "the difference received as inflated cost of project works for the relocation of engineering networks was used by A, as the sole founder of the LLP, for personal purposes, acquiring two expensive vehicles, 2012 Toyota Land Cruiser 200, purchased on 24 July 2014, for KZT 15 788 000 (the car had already been sold to a bona fide purchaser by the time of sentencing), and a 2012 Mercedes-Benz SL 500, bought on 15 September 2014, for KZT 22 005 000". The court held that the Mercedes-Benz SL 500 was purchased with funds obtained from A's criminal activities (committed embezzlement) and, therefore, is subject to confiscation for the benefit of the state.

Source: Court verdict in the case No. 7198-20-2-1/72, dated 28 May 2021.

This approach appears to be fully consistent with internationally recognised approaches to confiscation of proceeds of crime.

4.3 Confiscation of derivative income

In the 48 judicial verdicts reviewed, there were no instances of the confiscation of derivative (indirect) proceeds from corruption crimes, profits, or other benefits derived from them during the period from 2021 to 2023. It aligns with the findings of the country monitoring conducted by the OECD after that period (2024[9]), revealing that the country did not provide any examples of confiscation of derivative proceeds from corruption.

However, it appears that the current wording of the relevant legal provisions includes key elements that should permit the confiscation of at least derivative proceeds from corruption crimes. Thus, Paras 1 and 2 of Part 2 of Article 48 of the CC (2014[5]) stipulate that confiscation applies to money and other property:

- Obtained as a result of committing a criminal offense, along with any income from that property, except for which is to be returned to its lawful owner.
- Into which, property obtained as a result of committing a criminal offense, as well as income from that property, has been partially or fully transformed or converted.

It would be advisable to enhance the existing formulation by including a reference to any other benefits (beyond profits) derived from such proceeds.

Box 4.2. Failure to confiscate indirect benefit from a corruption offense

The owner and manager of a LLP was convicted of active bribery for paying bribes to two inspectors from the Transport Control Department to facilitate the transportation of cargo with violations of cargo parameters, avoid administrative fines for the drivers of her company, and generally protect her business. The two inspectors from the Transport Control Department were convicted of passive bribery.

The court ruled to confiscate the value of the undiscovered objects of the crime (the bribes) from the recipients (the public officials). However, the issue of confiscating indirect benefits from corruption from the manager of the LLP was not raised by anyone in the case. Specifically, this concerns the sums of administrative fines that were not imposed by the state for violations of cargo parameters during her business operations, despite the systematic nature of these violations.

Such approaches to identifying and confiscating any benefits from corrupt crimes, including indirect benefits, should be implemented in practice. A positive aspect highlighted in this case is that the court ordered the confiscation of the amounts related to the undiscovered tools of crime.

Source: Court verdict in the case No. 5910-22-00-1/297, dated 7 March 2023.

4.4 Confiscation of mixed proceeds

According to Article 31(5) of the UNCAC (United Nations, 2004[3]), if proceeds of crime have been intermingled with property acquired from legitimate sources, such property may be confiscated up to the assessed value of the intermingled proceeds.

The CC (2014[5]) and CPC (2014[6]) do not provide for the concept of mixed proceeds of crime. Mixed proceeds were confiscated by none of the 48 court verdicts for the period from 2021 to 2023. It is in line with the findings of the Baseline Report of the Fifth Round of Monitoring of Anti-Corruption Reforms in Kazakhstan (OECD, 2024[9]), which states that in 2023, there were no cases of confiscation of mixed proceeds of corruption offenses and profits from them in Kazakhstan.

Interviews with investigators and prosecutors conducted as part of this study revealed that the issue of mixed assets, where proceeds of crime are often mingled with legal income, poses significant challenges in practice, particularly concerning mixed corporate or business assets. Respondents emphasised the need for legislative recognition of this concept, along with rules for the confiscation of such proceeds. Furthermore, there is a call for subsequent training of law enforcement officers and judges to ensure correct application in practice. In this regard, it is recommended that the legislation of Kazakhstan include provisions for the confiscation of mixed proceeds of corruption, based on international standards and best practices.

4.5 Value-based confiscation

Value-based (equivalent) confiscation is a legal instrument whereby, if there is no actual possibility of confiscating illegally obtained assets (due to them being misplaced, alienated, etc.), other property whose value corresponds to the value of the proceeds from the corruption offense, along with any profits or other benefits derived from it, shall be subject to confiscation.

According to Part 3 of Article 48 of the CC (Republic of Kazakhstan, 2014[5]), if confiscation of a specific object specified in Parts 1 and 2 of Article 48 is impossible at the time a court decision is made due to its use, sale, or for other reasons, the court decision shall instead order the confiscation of a sum of money equal to the value of that object.

Analysis of the judicial practice has indicated that in practice, the equivalent confiscation is primarily applied by the courts of Kazakhstan in cases of conviction for passive bribery. Usually, courts use the following wording: "to recover from the defendant the value of the undiscovered item of bribe KZT (value of bribe)". However, there are a significant number of instances where courts do not decide on the recovery of the undiscovered item of a bribe in similar cases (for example, cases No. 5910-23-00-1/46, No. 1910-21-00-1/257 and No. 3111-21-00-1/375).

In some cases, the court decides to recover from the defendant "the value of the undiscovered bribe object" while simultaneously removing the seizure of their property, citing that "its criminal origin has not been proved". For example, in case No. 1956-21-00-1/15, the court ruled to recover from the defendant the value of the undiscovered bribe object (KZT 24 000) and to return KZT 22 200 seized from him during the pre-trial investigation. Thus, courts, instead of applying Part 3 of Article 48 of the CC (2014[5]), which is seemingly applicable to such situations, return the seized assets to the defendants. In such circumstances, applying Part 3 of Article 48 of the CC would ensure guaranteed execution of the decision regarding the recovery of the value of the undiscovered item of bribe.

A slightly different approach was applied by a court in the verdict in another case. A defendant was convicted of taking bribes totalling KZT 5 333 000 (approximately USD 10 800). During the investigation, the defendant was searched, resulting in the seizure of money amounting to USD 11 001 and KZT 1 036 700. In the court ruling, the court decided "to recover for the state" from the defendant the undiscovered item of the bribe in the amount of KZT 5 333 000 (approximately USD 10 800), and chose not to impose confiscation under Article 48 of the CC (2014[5]). The court reasoned that "since it has not been established that the money, seized during the search, is an object of bribery or obtained by criminal means, the court, by virtue of Article 48 of the CC, cannot convert it into state income, as requested by the defendant's counsel". The court also held that, based on Article 166 of CPC (2014[6]), it deemed it necessary to confiscate the money belonging to the defendant, seized during the search, to enforce the sentence. The reasoning behind the court's reference to Article 166 of CPC (which addresses civil claims in criminal proceedings, typically not relevant in bribery cases) instead of Part 3 of Article 48 of the CC remains unclear.

In other categories of cases (embezzlement, abuse of official powers), courts mainly issue verdicts "to recover material damage to the state income", while the received benefit from such crimes is not identified, the use of received income is not monitored, part 3 of Article 48 of the CC (2014[5]) is not applied (the condition of the CC that confiscation is impossible due to the use, sale of property or for any other reason is not checked and not applied), the equivalence of the received income/benefit is not analysed, and compensation is not applied. This data was confirmed by findings of the country monitoring that covered 2023 (OECD[9]) – Kazakhstan did not provide any examples of application of confiscation of the equivalent of instruments or proceeds of corruption offenses for 2023.

Only the verdict in case No. 7198-20-2-1/72, dated 28 May 2021, provided for equivalent confiscation in its international legal sense. The court confiscated from the defendant, A., with reference to Part 2 and Part 3 of Article 48 of the CC (2014[5]), the equivalent value of the car Toyota Land Cruiser 200 acquired as a result of committing a corruption offense (embezzlement). The court's verdict substantiated that A., being the sole founder of a LLP, used the received difference of the cost of design works on removal of engineering networks for his personal needs, having purchased two expensive cars, including Toyota Land Cruiser 200, bought on 24 July 2014 for KZT 15 788 000. The court further noted that the said car was subsequently (in 2018 and 2019) resold several times and ruled that "considering that [the said car] was repeatedly sold to actually bona fide purchasers, the court considers it necessary to recover the value of the sold car in monetary equivalent, which totals KZT 15 788 000, from A. to the state income". Such judicial practice appears to be fully consistent with the internationally recognised approaches to confiscation of the equivalent of the proceeds of crime.

Representatives of non-governmental stakeholders interviewed noted that law enforcement and courts do not apply equivalent confiscation and could not recall such cases in corruption cases that they were aware of, particularly high-level corruption cases.

Interviews with investigators, prosecutors, and judges revealed that opinions on the possibility of applying equivalent confiscation in practice vary considerably. Some investigators and prosecutors believe that equivalent confiscation works in practice in Kazakhstan (mostly referring to decisions on the return of undiscovered bribe items to the state), while others believe that if the property was acquired before the crime was committed, it cannot be confiscated in any way, even under the equivalent confiscation regime, and that such confiscation would be, in their opinion, unfair. They believe that sole dwellings and legitimate assets cannot be confiscated, and that illegal assets should automatically be those acquired after or during the commission of the offense charged. It appears that the problem most likely lies in the lack of practitioners' familiarity with international norms and standards on equivalent confiscation, and it is recommended that this gap be addressed through capacity-building measures (training activities).

4.6 Confiscation of property of informed third parties

The UNCAC (United Nations, 2004[3]) does not contain any detailed rules on the application of confiscation to assets belonging to informed third parties. In accordance with Article 31(9) of the Convention, the provisions of this article shall not be interpreted in such a way as to prejudice the rights of bona fide third parties.

Much more developed provisions are contained in the Directives of the European Union in the relevant area, in particular the Directive (EU) 2024/1260 of the European Parliament and of the Council of 24 April 2024 on asset recovery and confiscation (European Union, 2024[7]). Although it is not binding for Kazakhstan, this can serve as an example of best practices. According to Article 13 of the Directive, EU member states must implement measures to allow for the confiscation of income or property transferred, directly or indirectly, by a suspect or accused person to a third party or acquired by a third party from the suspect or accused.

Confiscation is permissible when a domestic court determines that the relevant third parties knew or should have known that the transfer's purpose was to evade confiscation. Relevant indicators include: (a) the transfer or acquisition occurred without payment or for an amount significantly lower than the market value of the property, or (b) the property was transferred to close relatives while effectively remaining under the control of the suspect. These provisions must not affect the rights of legitimate third parties. Furthermore, under Article 24(7) of the Directive (European Union, 2024[7])., third parties maintain the right to claim recognition of ownership or other property rights, including in cases covered by Article 13.

As defined in Part 1 of Article 48 of the CC (2014[5]), one object of confiscation may include property owned by the convicted person or items that are instruments used for committing a crime. Para 5 of Part 2 of Article 48 of the CC specifies that confiscation can include instruments, means, and proceeds of crime that the convicted person has transferred to others. However, this key article does not provide detailed circumstances or grounds for confiscation from third parties, which may limit its application.

First, this definition may limit the scope of application of that provision regarding property owned by individuals who are neither suspects nor accused. Problems may arise when property is alienated before seizure, a common occurrence in corruption cases after the investigation has been started.

Second, the current legal framework may hinder the effective confiscation of assets owned by "informed third parties" or nominal owners. It is increasingly common for public officials, aware of corruption risks, to attempt to conceal their ill-gotten gains using intermediaries. Unfortunately, the Kazakhstani legal framework may not be sufficiently robust to address the confiscation of such assets, despite the provisions found in Para 5 of Part 2 of Article 48 of the CC (2014[5]).

This creates loopholes, as property may be transferred by individuals who are not yet convicted at the time of transfer, or actual transfers might not occur at all if assets are immediately registered to a front individual (nominee). Such loopholes undermine the effectiveness of confiscation laws.

The authorities indicate that when the criminal prosecution body identifies income derived from criminally obtained property, including property held by third parties, this leads to the registration of a criminal case under Article 218 or 218-1 of the CC (2014[5]), which addresses money laundering. The sanctions outlined in these articles allow for the confiscation of property, including the proceeds from criminally obtained assets. This serves as an additional method for confiscating property transferred to the nominal or actual ownership of corrupt officials.

Criminal law provides certain guarantees for bona fide third parties. Specifically, Part 3 of Article 113 of CPC (2014[6]) states that the relevance of the property to the subject of confiscation must be established. This means that to apply confiscation, it is necessary to prove that the property was obtained illegally, either through committing a criminal offense or as a result of the proceeds from such property. Additionally, it must be shown that the property was used, or intended to be used, as an instrument or means of committing a criminal offense. The Supreme Court of Kazakhstan has clarified (2015[14]) that, when deciding on the confiscation of property, including property registered to third parties, courts must necessarily verify the evidence that substantiates the origin of the property and the means with which it was acquired.

Article 118 of CPC (2014[6]) provides detailed provisions regarding the resolution of “the issue of material evidence.” According to Part 3 of Article 118 of CPC, when a court decides to terminate a criminal case or issue a sentence, it must address the status of material evidence. Specifically, if instruments or means of committing a criminal offense belong to a person who did not know, or should not have known, that their property was being used illegally, that property should be returned to them. Additionally, money and other property obtained by criminal means or funded through such means, excluding property and proceeds from criminal activity, should also be returned.

If there is a dispute over ownership of these items, it must be resolved through civil proceedings.

However, this provision applies only to material evidence. Not all instruments and proceeds of crime qualify as such and should not be treated as material evidence for the purposes of criminal confiscation. Additionally, the legal standards that govern criminal confiscation will always take priority.

Para 1-1 of Part 3 of Article 118 of CPC (2014[6]) specifies that third parties may only have their instruments and means of committing a crime returned if they were unaware of the illicit use of their property. In contrast, Para 4 of Part 4 of Article 118 of CPC addresses money and other property obtained criminally but fails to provide the same criteria for returning items to their rightful owners. This part mandates that such property be returned to the state, except for property and proceeds that are not subject to confiscation.

The Supreme Court of Kazakhstan, in its Normative Decision № 4 (2015[14]), clarified these provisions, stating: "When handling material evidence, the court must determine ownership and whether the owner was aware of the illegal use of their property. If the owner did not know and should not have known about the unlawful use, the property shall be returned to them”. This clarification also applies to instruments of crime as material evidence but does not pertain to assets that are proceeds of crime.

Ultimately, the regulatory framework governing the confiscation of property from informed third parties, both natural and legal persons, remains a legislative concern. This issue requires a legislative update to align with international standards and best practices in this area.

The existing regime for third-party confiscation in Kazakhstan was already evaluated by the OECD, covering the period from 2014 to 2016. The relevant monitoring report (OECD, 2017[8]) recommended that the country allow confiscation from third parties who knew or should have known about the criminal origin of property. Additionally, it called for protections for bona fide purchasers of property subject to confiscation.

In 2015, Kazakhstan amended Article 48 of the CC (2014[5]) to include property transferred by a convicted person to others. This change partially addresses the IAP recommendation for confiscation from third parties. Furthermore, in its September 2016 Interim Report, Kazakhstan referenced civil law provisions (namely, Article 261 of the Civil Code (1994[15]) concerning bona fide purchasers). However, these civil law provisions did not seem applicable to confiscation proceedings under criminal law.

The report subsequently recommended that Kazakhstan legislate further measures to facilitate confiscation from third parties aware of a property's criminal origin, as well as continue to protect bona fide purchasers of such property.

The Baseline Report of the Fifth Round of Monitoring of Anti-Corruption Reforms in Kazakhstan (OECD, 2024[9]) found that, in 2023, there were no instances of confiscation of instruments or proceeds from corruption offenses transferred to informed third parties. While a few cases of third-party property confiscation appeared in court verdicts, they do not conform to internationally recognised standards regarding confiscation.

Analysis of 48 court verdicts, issued from 2021 to 2023, revealed that only two cases involved confiscation of assets acquired in the names of third parties, such as relatives and friends of the defendant. In both cases, the courts did not verify whether the third parties were aware of the criminal origins of the assets or if the defendants had actual control over the assets. Both cases pertained to high-level corruption, but only one resulted in the confiscation of assets related to a high-ranking official's close associates.

Box 4.3. Confiscation from third parties: Case 1

On 1 February 2021, a court convicted an individual X, the Chairman of the unit of a public body, along with 21 other individuals, of embezzlement. The court found that during the commission of the crime, the defendants A, B and C acquired property using money obtained through criminal means, which is subject to confiscation for state revenue.

Specifically, B acquired two vehicles:

- a "Land Rover Range Rover Sport," purchased on 17 November 2018, in the name of D,
- a "Mercedes-Benz S500," purchased on 23 November 2018, in the name of E.

However, the verdict did not clarify the relationships between D and E and the convicted businessman B. Furthermore, it failed to explain the circumstances under which the cars were registered in their names, their awareness of this registration, and any evidence connecting the vehicles to the criminal activities mentioned, aside from the timing of their purchase.

In the same ruling, the court decided to lift the arrest on an apartment belonging to the defendant F, as it was found to have been purchased by his parents. The verdict did not provide a rationale for why this apartment was not confiscated to secure compensation for F's share in the embezzlement. Additionally, there were no references to Article 48 of the CC (2014[5]) or Article 118 of CPC (2014[6]) concerning the confiscation of third-party property.

Source: Court verdict in the case No. 7511-20-00-1/223, dated 1 February 2021.

Below is another example from the judicial practice of Kazakhstan regarding confiscation from third parties.

Box 4.4. Confiscation from third parties: Case 2

In 2023, the court convicted a Vice-Minister of Kazakhstan of abuse of office. During the court hearing, the Vice-Minister admitted that after his dismissal, he acquired shares in 13 companies.

With the dividends from one of these investments, he purchased a 2021 "Mercedes-Benz Maybach S580" and a 2021 "Bentley Bentayga V8," registering the vehicles in the names of his father and mother-in-law. He also acquired land plot No. 24, adjacent to plots No. 23 and No. 27, with residential buildings on them. New land plot was registered in the name of his father. These plots collectively constituted a single territory encompassing the residence in which the Vice-Minister lived.

Court ruled that, since this property was obtained during the commission of crimes and funded by illicit means, it was necessary to confiscate it for state revenue. The Vice-Minister acknowledged that the vehicles, registered to his father and mother-in-law, actually belonged to him. For the land plots No. 23 and No. 27, no evidence was presented other than the fact that the Vice-Minister lived in the house located there.

Source: Court verdict in the case No. 7135-23-00-1/338, dated 27 October 2023.

In the aforementioned example, the criteria used by the court to decide on the confiscation of property from third parties, specifically two vehicles and two land plots, are not clearly discernible. It appears that the primary factor was the acquisition of this property during the commission of the crime, rather than the identities of the legal registrants or the circumstances of the registration. Additionally, the subjective views of the de jure owners regarding that registration were not considered.

An analysis of judicial practices generally supports the earlier conclusions about the shortcomings of the current legislation of Kazakhstan concerning the criminal confiscation of property owned by informed third parties, whether individuals or legal entities. None of the reviewed verdicts indicated instances of criminal confiscation from legal entities as third parties. Moreover, there are no maintained official statistics on criminal confiscations involving third parties, either natural or legal persons.

Interviews conducted for this research with legal practitioners – Investigators, prosecutors and judges, as well as representatives from interested non-governmental organisations, confirmed ongoing issues with this type of criminal confiscation in practice. Law enforcement officials noted that government officials often avoid registering property in their own names or the names of their close relatives. They reported that "officials submit income declarations, and there are declarations of their family members (spouses, children), but no one declares assets in their own name or in the name of close relatives. Any official has many close associates ("cronies") who rely on them".

It was also emphasised that, in cases involving the seizure and confiscation of property from third parties, establishing a criminal connection is essential. Previously, this was demonstrated by properties being acquired after the commission of a crime; however, recent court rulings now require prosecutors to prove a specific link to a crime. If an official registers property in the name of a driver, the act of "transfer of property" must be proven. It was noted that while proving this connection is generally not a problem at the central office, regional courts may occasionally reject such claims.

All practitioners interviewed were of the same opinion that, in practice, challenges arise when applying property seizure and confiscation to affiliated third parties, such as drivers and friends of officials. Representatives from non-governmental organisations remarked that they could not recall any high-profile corruption cases that involved the confiscation of assets registered in the names of third parties. They further noted that in ongoing criminal investigations, "no one seems to care when assets have been transferred to classmates, friends, and so on".

4.7 Procedure for criminal non-conviction-based confiscation

Kazakhstan's legislation provides for a special procedure for pre-conviction confiscation proceedings in the Chapter 71 of Section 15 of CPC (2014[6]). A detailed analysis of the legal regulation of such confiscation is provided in subchapter 2.2 of this study.

The analysis of court practice for 2021–2023 does not reveal any court decisions on confiscation of criminally obtained property in cases of corruption offenses before conviction (in accordance with the procedure of Chapter 71, Section 15 of CPC (2014[6])). This is confirmed by the Baseline Report of the Fifth Round of Monitoring of Anti-Corruption Reforms in Kazakhstan (OECD, 2024[9]), which did not identify cases of non-conviction-based confiscation of instruments and proceeds of corruption offenses in Kazakhstan in 2023. Practitioners interviewed for the purposes of this study were aware of cases where this tool has been used in other categories of cases (theft, smuggling, etc.), but noted that these are still rather rare in practice. There are no separate statistics available to distinguish confiscation data in such cases.

The interviews conducted during this study confirmed the existence of issues in practice with the application of this type of confiscation. Thus, investigators noted that initiating confiscation proceedings without conviction following the termination of criminal proceedings on the basis of Para 11 of Part 1 of Article 35 of CPC (2014[6]) (death of a defendant, except when the proceedings are necessary for the rehabilitation of the deceased) is challenging in practice. It requires the consent of relatives, and relatives often do not agree with the termination of the case and demand further legal proceedings seeking rehabilitation of the deceased. This is often related to issues of inheritance, as the relatives want to inherit the seized expensive property. It also involves concerns about their future employment, since the termination of the criminal case due to death is a non-exonerating ground that may impact the employment rights of these relatives. Virtually all practitioners recognised during the interviews that pre-trial confiscation does not function normally in practice in Kazakhstan, in particular in cases of corruption offenses. In this regard, the opinions of non-governmental stakeholders were in full agreement.

Practitioners noted that pre-conviction confiscation is not applied on other grounds (a defendant is on internationally wanted list, termination of criminal case due to amnesty or due to expiration of statute of limitations). This is due to courts being extremely reluctant to apply it in practice on other grounds. Practitioners also noted that if a wanted person (in criminal proceedings) or a deceased person (in criminal proceedings for their exoneration) is later acquitted (on any grounds), then assets confiscated in pre-conviction confiscation proceedings will have to be returned to that person (in the former case) or to their relatives (in the latter case). Thus, such confiscation proceedings are directly dependent on the outcome of the underlying criminal proceedings.

The analysis of the provisions of Chapter 71 of Section 15 of CPC (2014[6]) and the results of interviews allow for the conclusion that the most probable reasons for the ineffectiveness of the existing regime of non-conviction-based confiscation in Kazakhstan are as follows:

- The criminal confiscation of property obtained through illegal means is dependent on the primary criminal proceedings against the individual before a verdict is issued. In cases of the individual's death, relatives typically insist on the continuation of these proceedings, especially when substantial property is involved. If the individual is acquitted for any reason, the confiscation of property may be subject to review and cancellation.

- The standard of proof in confiscation proceedings requires a "beyond reasonable doubt" threshold. The elements that must be proven for confiscation are the same as those needed for the conviction of the individual for the crime, as outlined in Part 2 of Article 113 and Article 668 of CPC (2014[6]).
- There is a limited scope of application for confiscation. It applies only to property obtained illegally, while tools or means used to commit the crime may not qualify. Additionally, the equivalent of criminal proceeds does not fall under this category.
- There are challenges in applying confiscation to the property of third parties. In such cases, it is necessary to contest transactions in civil proceedings, which can significantly complicate and prolong the process. According to Part 3 of Article 668 of CPC (2014[6]), if there is evidence of the suspect or accused hiding property by transferring it to others, the investigator must submit a motion to the prosecutor. This motion requests a decision on whether to file a civil lawsuit to invalidate transactions (such as sales, gifts, leases, or trusts) in the interest of the state or victims.

It is recommended to consider introducing special rules that allow for the confiscation of criminally derived property regardless of the status of the principal criminal case. This could include provisions for temporary confiscation while the criminal case is pending, to prevent further loss or decline in the value of the seized property.

Furthermore, it would be advisable to strengthen the legal provisions regarding the protection of property rights for individuals whose property is subject to confiscation without a conviction. The current CPC (Republic of Kazakhstan, 2014[6]) stipulates that the prosecutor who filed the motion participates in the court hearing (Part 3 of Article 669 of CPC). Other individuals may also be summoned to provide testimony regarding the motion if requested by the defence counsel of the suspect or accused (Part 4 of Article 669 of CPC). However, the provisions of Chapter 71 of Section 15 of CPC do not explicitly require the summoning of the defence counsel or attorney of the individual whose property is at risk of confiscation without a conviction.

This deficiency was also identified during the Fourth round of monitoring of Kazakhstan under IAP. The monitoring report (OECD, 2017[8]) highlighted the need to strengthen guarantees for protecting the interests of individuals whose property is confiscated prior to a conviction. Specifically, it should be mandated that the defence counsel of the suspect or accused must be summoned to the court hearing. Additionally, the absence of these individuals, provided they have been properly notified, should not hinder the judicial proceedings or the consideration of the confiscation motion. This shortcoming in the legal framework needs to be addressed.

The legal institution of criminal confiscation prior to the issuance of a verdict in Kazakhstan has the potential to serve as a model of best practices in the Central Asian region. However, effective implementation of this mechanism in practice is essential. If the recommendations from this study are followed and improvements are made to this tool, the likelihood of its successful application will significantly increase.

4.8 Extended confiscation in criminal proceedings

The UNCAC (United Nations, 2004[3]) contains a soft recommendation urging State Parties to consider establishing a requirement that individuals who have committed a crime demonstrate the lawful origin of such alleged proceeds of crime or other property subject to confiscation, to the extent that such a requirement aligns with the fundamental principles of their domestic laws and the nature of judicial and other proceedings (Article 31(8).

At the same time, the Directive (EU) 2024/1260 of 24 April 2024, regarding the recovery of assets and confiscation (European Union, 2024[7]) explicitly obliges all EU member states to implement criminal extended confiscation into their legislation (Article 14). According to this provision, EU member states must take necessary measures to ensure the confiscation, in whole or in part, of property belonging to an individual convicted of a crime, where such property is directly or indirectly related to the obtaining of economic benefits and where the national court concludes that such property has been acquired through criminal conduct. In determining whether the disputed property was obtained from criminal behaviour, all circumstances of the case should be considered, including specific facts and available evidence, such as the fact that the value of such property does not correspond to the lawful income of the convicted individual. For the purposes of this article, the term "crime" should include at least (criminal) offenses listed in Paras 1–3 of Article 2, in cases where they entail a penalty of imprisonment for a term of not less than four years. Additionally, Article 16 of the Directive provides for the confiscation of unexplained wealth associated with criminal behaviour as an alternative (i.e., these are two distinct legal instruments; thus, the institution of extended criminal confiscation should not be confused with civil confiscation as provided by the Law of the Republic of Kazakhstan "On the Return of Illegally Acquired Assets to the State", dated 12 July 2023 (2023[10]).

Even not being binding for Kazakhstan, the EU Directive 2014/42/EU of the European Parliament and of the Council on the freezing and confiscation of instruments and proceeds of crime in the European Union (European Union, 2014[4]) may serve as an example of best practices. It should also be noted that the EU Directive establishes minimum necessary standards for EU member states in the relevant area, and countries may go further by establishing even stricter regimes of extended criminal confiscation. Among the countries of Central Asia and Eastern Partnership, extended criminal confiscation is provided for in the Criminal Code of the Republic of Moldova (Article 106-1) (Republic of Moldova, 2002[16]).

The GRECO stated (2022[11]) that neither the CC nor CPC provide for the transfer of the burden of proof in cases of criminal confiscation. GRECO noted that it is increasingly common for states to have legislation that stipulates that in criminal confiscation proceedings, where an individual has been convicted of a profit-generating crime and it has been proven that they possess property for which there is no identified lawful explanation, that individual bears the burden of proving that the property is not criminal proceeds. A conviction and the absence of an identified lawful explanation for the sources of the property, which the offender is proven to own, are circumstances from which, when considered together, it may reasonably be inferred that such property constitutes proceeds of crime. In such a situation, the requirement that the offender was required to demonstrate the legitimacy of the source of origin of the property does not appear unreasonable. After all, the origin of their property is a fact entirely within their knowledge. Moreover, the allocation of the burden of proof in this way does not necessarily entail the application of any particular standard of proof to the offender. In this regard, GRECO recommended that Kazakhstan consider reviewing the burden of proof required in relation to conviction in order to provide a better opportunity to apply confiscation in corruption cases effectively.

The majority of law enforcement practitioners interviewed agreed on the feasibility of implementing the institution of extended confiscation within the criminal process, whereby the burden of proof for the lawful origin of property could be placed on the convicted individual in cases involving profit-generating crimes. Many practitioners believe that this would be highly beneficial for them and consider such an approach consistent with international standards. There were also opinions expressed that Kazakhstan is not yet ready for the approaches outlined in the Directive (EU) 2024/1260 of the European Parliament and of the Council of 24 April 2024 on asset recovery and confiscation (European Union, 2024[7]), and that the implementation of extended criminal confiscation should occur gradually, after the launch of a universal income and property declaration system for citizens (scheduled for 2025–2026). Arguments were presented that "since Soviet times, accountability for citizens' incomes has been lost" and that "during that time there were undeclared but lawful incomes," which would be difficult to prove. However, overall, the idea of the feasibility of introducing such a tool (criminal extended confiscation) in one form or another received support from all.

The analysis of the current legislation of Kazakhstan regarding criminal confiscation, international standards in this area, best practices from EU countries and the region, reports from international organisations, and the outcomes of interviews with law enforcement practitioners, judges, and governmental stakeholders allow for the recommendation that the authorities of the Kazakhstan consider the possibility of incorporating the institution of extended criminal confiscation into its legislation and practice based on the provisions of Directive (EU) 2024/1260 of 24 April 2024 regarding asset recovery and confiscation (European Union, 2024[7]), as well as best practices from countries in the region.

4.9 Recovery of assets from abroad through criminal confiscation

In the responses to the Questionnaire for this study, it was indicated that from 2021 to 2023, there was not a single instance of confiscation and return of assets to Kazakhstan from abroad through criminal confiscation. Similarly, the responses provided in the Questionnaire revealed no requests for legal assistance related to the application of criminal confiscation to property abroad during this period, including in criminal cases concerning corruption (enforcement abroad of final court decisions from Kazakhstan regarding criminal confiscation.)

These findings are supported by the earlier OECD report (OECD, 2024[9]), which noted the absence of incidents involving the return of corrupt income from abroad in 2023. However, the Report revealed information from authorities indicating that, during 2021 and 2022, two requests for mutual legal assistance were sent regarding in a criminal case to the Swiss Confederation. Kazakh authorities sought the enforcement of a default judgement (in absentia) rendered by a court in Kazakhstan on 29 December 2020, convicting of embezzlement, money laundering and other crimes an individual who had fled justice and was residing in Canada. The court found that the defendant embezzled and laundered assets belonging to a national company amounting to KZT 11 billion. The defendant was sanctioned with confiscation of funds totalling EUR 9 661 948.79 and USD 2 448 977.48, located in Switzerland. As of 2024, these requests for legal assistance were still under consideration by Swiss authorities.

The analysis of 48 court verdicts concerning corruption offenses from 2021 to 2023 revealed a lack of decisions regarding the criminal confiscation of property belonging to convicted individuals or informed third parties located abroad.

Interviews with practitioners and non-governmental stakeholders conducted for this study confirmed the absence of practical instances of recovering proceeds of corruption from abroad through criminal confiscation in recent years. Investigators and prosecutors highlighted the fairly long execution of requests for legal assistance abroad as a primary issue in this area. However, the absence of verdicts involving the confiscation of corrupt proceeds from abroad over the past three years at national level suggests deeper underlying issues.

It appears that the root of the challenge lies in the current design of the criminal confiscation system in Kazakhstan, which does not fully align with minimal international standards or best practices in the region. The recommendations provided below for enhancing the country's criminal confiscation regime, if properly implemented, are expected to significantly improve the situation regarding the seizure, confiscation and recovery of corrupt proceeds from abroad, particularly in cases involving high-level corruption.

Recommendations

- Ensure the autonomy of criminal non-conviction-based confiscation proceedings (Chapter 71 of Section 15 of CPC (2014[6])) so that they do not depend directly and automatically on the progress and outcomes of the primary criminal proceedings. The termination of the case against the individual or their acquittal in the primary proceedings should not entail the automatic cancellation of confiscation within the criminal non-conviction-based confiscation.
- Ensure that the legal framework for criminal non-conviction-based confiscation covers a broad range of objects, including instruments (tools and means) of the crime, proceeds from crimes, profits or other benefits derived from them, commingled proceeds, and value-based confiscation.
- Apply the criminal non-conviction-based confiscation framework effectively to assets registered in the names of informed third parties, without the necessity of resorting to legal remedies such as the annulment of transactions in civil proceedings.
- Formalise the concept of "instruments, tools, and means of committing a crime" as a mandatory object for confiscation, while ensuring a clear distinction between their confiscation and the disposition of material evidence.
- Formalise the concept of “proceeds from crime”—including direct and derivative proceeds, as well as any subsequent profits and benefits derived from them—as mandatory objects for confiscation, provided there is a proven link to the specific crime through which they were obtained. Additionally, ensure their confiscation is distinguished from the disposition of material evidence.
- Ensure that, during the prosecution of corruption offenses, instruments (tools and means) used to commit such crimes, direct and derivative proceeds, any subsequent profits and other benefits derived from the commission of corruption offenses are systematically identified, seized, and confiscated in practice, specifically in their capacity as such.
- Ensure a consistent transition in practice from the currently prevailing concept of "damage" from corruption crimes to the conceptualisation of corrupt income or benefits as objects of confiscation in cases of corruption offenses that generate such income or benefits, such as bribery, abuse of power, and embezzlement.
- Provide in legislation for the confiscation of mixed proceeds from crimes as a separate object, aiming to facilitate the confiscation of property corresponding to the assessed value of the associated criminal proceeds, including any subsequent profits and benefits derived therefrom.
- Enhance the capacity of investigators, prosecutors, and judges specialising in the prosecution and judicial review of corruption cases, ensuring that the confiscation of property (the value of which corresponds to the value of direct and indirect proceeds from corruption offenses), is systematically applied in practice.
- Include in the law detailed provisions on the criminal confiscation of property belonging to informed third parties (both individuals and legal entities). These provisions should include clear criteria for applying such confiscation and appropriate safeguards to protect the rights of genuine third parties.
- Ensure that during the prosecution of corruption offenses, assets registered in the names of nominal (informed) third parties, including in high-level corruption cases, are systematically identified, seized, and confiscated, while the rights of bona fide third parties are upheld in practice.

- Improve the legal framework for criminal non-conviction-based confiscation (Chapter 71 of Section 15 of CPC (2014[6])). This can be achieved by ensuring the autonomy of this process from the primary investigation. The relevant steps may include establishing a lighter burden of proof, limiting the elements to be proven, broadening the range of objects of confiscation (including instruments, direct and indirect proceeds from crimes, mixed proceeds, equivalents, etc.), ensuring effective confiscation of assets registered to informed third parties, and enhancing the right to protection for individuals whose property is considered for confiscation.
- Introduce the framework for extended criminal confiscation into the legislation of Kazakhstan based on the provisions of Directive (EU) 2024/1260 (2024[7]) regarding asset recovery and confiscation, as well as best practices from countries in the region.

5 Criminal sanctions, statutes of limitations and immunities

This chapter outlines the types of penalties for criminal offenses, provides statistics on their application. It analyses gaps and shortcomings in the criminal sanctioning framework. Additionally, the chapter examines the practices and challenges in enforcing corruption offenses, particularly regarding the immunities enjoyed by high-level officials and the statutes of limitations.

5.1 Types of penalties

According to Article 39 of the CC (2014[5]), a penalty is defined as a measure of state coercion imposed by a court judgment. A penalty is applicable to an individual who has been found guilty of committing a criminal offense and consists of the deprivation or restriction of that individual's rights and freedoms as stipulated by the CC. The imposition of a penalty aims to restore social justice, exonerate the convicted individual, and prevent the commission of new criminal offenses by both the convicted individual and others. The purpose of the penalty is not to inflict physical suffering or undermine human dignity.

In accordance with Article 40 of the CC (2014[5]), an individual found guilty of committing a crime7 may be subjected to the following principal penalties: fine, corrective labour, community service, restriction of liberty, and imprisonment. For the commission of a misdemeanour, the following principal penalties may apply - fine, corrective labour, community service, arrest, and deportation of a foreigner or stateless person.

In addition to the principal penalties, an individual found guilty of committing a criminal offense may be subjected to the following additional penalties: confiscation of property, disqualification from holding a special, military, or honorary title, class rank, diplomatic status, qualification class, and state awards; prohibition on holding certain positions or engaging in specific activities; revocation of citizenship of Kazakhstan; and deportation of a foreigner or stateless person.

Furthermore, more detailed information is provided regarding the penalties that are most frequently imposed in practice for cases involving corruption offenses.

Imprisonment

Imprisonment involves isolating the convicted individual from society by placing them in a penitentiary facility. The term of imprisonment for offenses outlined in the CC ranges from six months to fifteen years. For particularly serious offenses, the term may extend to twenty years or life imprisonment. In cases of offenses by negligence, the term of imprisonment shall not exceed ten years. When substituting a fine, corrective labour, community service, or restriction of liberty with imprisonment, the term may be imposed for less than six months.

In the event of partial or total aggregation of terms of imprisonment when sentencing for multiple offenses (Part 5 of Article 71 and Part 5 of Article 77 of the CC (2014[5])), the maximum term of imprisonment shall not exceed twenty-five years, and when aggregating sentences, it shall not exceed thirty years. Life imprisonment may be imposed for the commission of particularly serious offenses. Life imprisonment shall not be imposed on individuals who committed the crime at an age below eighteen years, on women, or on men aged sixty-three years and older. Furthermore, life imprisonment may, through the mechanism of clemency, be commuted to a fixed-term imprisonment (Article 46 of the CC).

Restriction of liberty

Restriction of liberty consists of the establishment of probationary supervision over the convicted individual for a term ranging from six months to seven years and requiring their engagement in compulsory labour for one hundred hours annually throughout the duration of the penalty. This measure is served at the place of residence of the convicted individual, without isolation from society.

Probationary supervision is implemented by the authorised state body and, by court decision, includes the fulfilment by the convicted individual of the following obligations: not changing their permanent place of residence, employment, or study without notifying the supervising authority; not visiting specified locations;

undergoing treatment for designated disorders (illnesses); providing financial support to their family; and adhering to other obligations that facilitate the rehabilitation of the convicted individual and the prevention of further criminal offenses.

In cases of wilful evasion of the terms of restriction of liberty, the unfulfilled term may be replaced by imprisonment, calculated at the rate of one day of imprisonment for each day of restriction of liberty. When a lesser penalty than that prescribed for the given criminal offense is imposed, when a penalty is imposed for an incomplete crime, or when a penalty is substituted, the term of restriction of liberty may be set below the minimum limit established by Article 44 of the CC (2014[5]).

Confiscation of property

Confiscation of property as a measure of sanctioning (Article 48 of the CC (2014[5])) is described in detail in Chapter 2 of this study.

Fine

A fine is defined as a monetary penalty imposed within the limits established by the CC (2014[5]), calculated based on a specified number of monthly calculation indicators[8] as determined by the legislation of Kazakhstan in force at the time the criminal offense was committed, or in an amount that is a multiple of the sum or value of a bribe, the amount of money transferred, the value of property transferred, the value of stolen property, the amount of income received, or the amount of payments not remitted to the budget.

For misdemeanour, the fine is imposed within the range of twenty to two hundred monthly calculation indicators, whereas for crimes, the range is from two hundred to ten thousand monthly calculation indicators or an equivalent amount. The court determines the size and deadline for the payment of the fine, considering the severity of the criminal offense, the financial and family situation of the convicted individual, and their ability to earn wages or other income.

The deadline for the payment of the fine is calculated from the moment the judgment becomes final and cannot exceed three years as determined by the court's ruling. In cases of temporary deterioration in the financial situation of the convicted individual due to delays or non-payment of wages, temporary disability, job loss, or loss of income, the court may grant a deferment of payment for a period ranging from one month to one year. The period of deferment is not included in the calculation of the deadline for the payment of the fine established by the court.

In the event of non-payment of the fine within the established deadlines, the court's judgment must be enforced by coercive measures. The unpaid portion of the fine may be replaced by other types of penalties in the proportion established by the CC (2014[5]). When a lesser penalty than that prescribed for the given criminal offense is imposed, in the case of sentencing for an incomplete crime, or when substituting a penalty, the amount of the fine may be set below the minimum limit established by the Article 40 of the CC.

Deprivation of titles, awards and rights

When convicting an individual for the commission of a deliberate criminal offense, the court may revoke their special, military, honorary, or other titles, class ranks, diplomatic statuses, or qualification classes based on the nature of the offender's personality. In the case of a defendant who holds state awards of Kazakhstan, along with special, military, honorary, or other titles, class ranks, diplomatic statuses, or qualification classes conferred by the President of Kazakhstan, the court may submit a recommendation to the President for the revocation of those awards, titles, class ranks, diplomatic statuses, or qualification classes when rendering the judgment, particularly in cases of corruption offenses (Article 49 of the CC (2014[5])).

The penalty of prohibition from holding certain positions or engaging in specific activities consists of a ban on occupying specified positions in public service, local government bodies, financial organisations, or engaging in certain professional or other activities. This punishment is established for a term ranging from one year to ten years. For the commission of corruption offenses, the prohibition from holding certain positions or engaging in specific activities is mandatory and consists of a lifetime ban from holding positions in public service, as a judge, in local government bodies, the National Bank of Kazakhstan and its agencies, the authorised regulatory, supervisory, and oversight bodies of the financial market and financial organisations, as well as in state organisations and quasi-public sector entities.

This penalty may also be imposed in cases where it is not provided for in the relevant article of the Special Part of the CC as an additional penalty for the corresponding criminal offense, if, considering the nature and degree of its social danger and the personality of the offender, the court determines that it is impossible to allow that individual to retain the right to hold certain positions or engage in specific activities (Article 50 of the CC (2014[5])).

General principles and rules of sentencing

In accordance with Article 52 of the CC (2014[5]) (General Principles of Sentencing), an individual found guilty of committing a criminal offense shall be sentenced with a fair punishment within the limits established by the relevant article of the Special Part of the CC, considering the provisions of the General Part. The penalty imposed must be necessary and sufficient for the individual's rehabilitation and for the prevention of new criminal offenses. A more severe form of punishment out of those provided for the committed criminal offense may be imposed only if a less severe form is unable to achieve the objectives of punishment.

More severe penalty than that prescribed by the pertinent articles of the Special Part of the CC (2014[5]) for the committed act may be imposed based on the aggregation of criminal offenses or the aggregation of sentences in accordance with Articles 58 and 60 of the CC. The grounds for imposing a less severe punishment than that prescribed by the corresponding articles of the Special Part for the committed act are determined by Article 55 of the CC.

In determining the punishment, the court considers the nature and degree of the social danger of the criminal offense, the personality of the offender, including their behaviour before and after the commission of the offense, mitigating and aggravating circumstances, and the impact of the imposed penalty on the rehabilitation of the convicted individual and the living conditions of their family or dependents.

The circumstances that mitigate or aggravate criminal liability and penalties are outlined in Articles 54 and 55 of the CC (2014[5]), respectively. The commission of a criminal offense by an individual who has violated an oath (which public officials take upon entering service) constitutes an aggravating circumstance that affects both liability and the severity of the penalty.

Additionally, Article 55 of the CC (2014[5]) allows for the possibility of imposing a more lenient punishment than that prescribed for a particular criminal offense. According to Parts 4 and 5 of this Article, if there are exceptional circumstances related to the goal and motives of the act, the role of the convicted individual, their behaviour during or after the crime, and other circumstances that significantly reduce the act's social danger, the punishment may be set below the minimum limit prescribed by the corresponding article of the Special Part of the CC. The court may also impose a more lenient type of punishment than what is provided in the relevant article or refrain from imposing an additional punishment that is mandated under the law.

Exceptional circumstances can include individual mitigating factors or a combination of such factors. However, it is important to note that Part 8 of Article 55 of the CC (2014[5]), which outlines exceptions to these rules, does not apply to corruption offenses.

Conditional sentencing

Article 63 of the CC (2014[5]) provides that if, when imposing a sentence of imprisonment, the court concludes that the convicted individual can be rehabilitated without serving the sentence, it shall determine that the imposed sentence is conditional. When assigning a conditional sentence, the court must establish, according to the rules outlined in Part 2 of Article 44 of the CC, probationary supervision for the entire duration of the imposed sentence of imprisonment (Parts 1 and 3 of Article 63 of the CC).

According to Part 6 of Article 63 of the CC (2014[5]), a conditional sentence shall not be applied, in particular, in cases of conviction for a corruption offense.

5.2 Penalties for corruption offenses

In Kazakhstan, the law provides for the following sanctions for corruption offenses in the public sector.

Theft under Part 1 of Article 189 of the CC (2014[5]), which constitutes the basic offense, shall be punishable by a fine of up to one thousand monthly calculation indicators (MCI), or by corrective labour of the same amount, or by community service for a duration of up to eight hundred hours, or by restriction of freedom for a term not exceeding three years, or by imprisonment for the same term, with or without confiscation of property.

Theft under Part 2 of Article 189 of the CC (2014[5]), including acts committed by an individual utilizing their official position, shall be punishable by a fine of up to three thousand MCIs, or by corrective labour of the same amount, or by community service for a duration of up to one thousand hours, or by restriction of freedom for a term not exceeding four years, or by imprisonment for the same term, with confiscation of property and with deprivation of the right to hold certain positions or engage in specified activities for a term of up to three years, or without such deprivation.

Theft under Part 3 of Article 189 of the CC (2014[5]), including acts committed by a person authorised to perform public functions, or by a person equated to such, or by an official, or by a person holding a responsible government position, provided that such acts are committed in connection with the misuse of their official position as defined in Para 2, shall be punishable by restriction of freedom for a term of not less than two years and not more than seven years, or by imprisonment for the same term, with confiscation of property, and with deprivation of the right to hold certain positions or engage in specified activities for a term of up to six years, or without such deprivation. In the cases specified in Para 2, the penalty shall include a fine ranging from ten to twenty times the value of the stolen property, or imprisonment for a term of not less than two years and not more than seven years, with confiscation of property, and with a lifelong deprivation of the right to hold certain positions or engage in specific activities.

Theft under Para 4 of Article 189 of the CC (2014[5]) shall be punishable by imprisonment for a term of not less than seven years and not more than twelve years, with confiscation of property, and with a lifelong prohibition from holding certain positions or engaging in specific activities for a term of up to ten years, or without such prohibition. In the cases outlined in Para 2 of Part 3 of this article, it shall result in a lifelong deprivation of the right to hold certain positions or engage in specific activities.

Abuse of official authority under Part 1 of Article 361 of the CC (2014[5]), which constitutes the basic offense, is punishable by a fine of up to two thousand MCIs, or by corrective labour of the same amount, or by community service for a duration of up to six hundred hours, or by restriction of freedom for a term not exceeding two years, or by imprisonment for the same term, with confiscation of property and a lifelong prohibition from holding certain positions or engaging in specific activities.

Abuse of official power as defined in Part 2-1 of Article 361 of the CC (2014[5]), which pertains to the same act committed by an employee of a law enforcement agency, is punishable by a fine of up to four thousand

MCI, or by corrective labour of the same amount, or by community service for a duration of up to one thousand hours, or by restriction of freedom for a term not exceeding four years, or by imprisonment for the same term, with confiscation of property and a lifelong prohibition from holding certain positions or engaging in specific activities.

Abuse of official authority under Part 3 of Article 361 of the CC (2014[5]), committed by an individual holding a responsible government position, is punishable by a fine of up to five thousand MCIs, or by corrective labour of the same amount, or by community service for a duration of up to one thousand two hundred hours, or by restriction of freedom for a term not exceeding five years, or by imprisonment for the same term, with confiscation of property and a lifelong prohibition from holding certain positions or engaging in specific activities.

Abuse of official authority under Part 4 of Article 361 of the CC (2014[5]), including acts committed by a judge or a person holding a responsible government position within a law enforcement agency, is punishable by restriction of freedom for a term not exceeding seven years or by imprisonment for the same term, with confiscation of property and a lifelong prohibition from holding certain positions or engaging in specific activities.

Receiving a bribe under Part 1 of Article 366 of the CC (2014[5]), which constitutes the basic offense, is punishable by a fine ranging from twenty times to fifty times the amount of the bribe or by imprisonment for a term not exceeding five years, with confiscation of property and a lifelong prohibition from holding certain positions or engaging in specific activities.

For aggravated forms of passive bribery, the CC (2014[5]) stipulates the following penalties: under Part 2, Article366, a fine ranging from fifty times to sixty times the amount of the bribe or imprisonment for a term from three to seven years, with confiscation of property and a lifelong prohibition from holding certain positions or engaging in specific activities; Under Part 3 of Article 366, a fine ranging from sixty times to seventy times the amount of the bribe or imprisonment for a term from seven to twelve years, with confiscation of property and a lifelong prohibition from holding certain positions or engaging in specific activities; and under Part 4 of Article 366, a fine ranging from seventy times to eighty times the amount of the bribe or imprisonment for a term from ten to fifteen years, with confiscation of property and a lifelong prohibition from holding certain positions or engaging in specific activities.

Giving a bribe under Part 1 of Article 367 of the CC (2014[5]), which constitutes a basic offense, is punishable by a fine ranging from twenty times to thirty times the amount of the bribe or by imprisonment for a term not exceeding five years, with confiscation of property and a lifelong prohibition from holding certain positions or engaging in specific activities.

For aggravated forms of active bribery the CC (2014[5]) specifies the following penalties: under Part 2, Article 367, a fine ranging from thirty times to forty times the amount of the bribe or imprisonment for a term from three to seven years, with confiscation of property and a lifelong prohibition from holding certain positions or engaging in specific activities; under Part 3 of Article 367 of the CC, a fine ranging from forty times to fifty times the amount of the bribe or imprisonment for a term from seven to twelve years, with confiscation of property and a lifelong prohibition from holding certain positions or engaging in specific activities, and under Part 4 of Article 367 of the CC, a fine ranging from fifty times to sixty times the amount of the bribe or imprisonment for a term from ten to fifteen years, with confiscation of property and a lifelong prohibition from holding certain positions or engaging in specific activities.

Mediation in bribery under Part 1 of Article 368 of the CC (2014[5]), which constitutes the basic offense, is punishable by a fine ranging from ten times to twenty times the amount of the bribe or by imprisonment for a term not exceeding three years, with confiscation of property and a lifelong prohibition from holding certain positions or engaging in specific activities. Mediation under Part 2 of Article 368 of the CC, including acts committed by a person utilizing their official position, is punishable by a fine ranging from twenty times to thirty times the amount of the bribe or by imprisonment for a term not exceeding six years, with confiscation of property and a lifelong prohibition from holding certain positions or engaging in specific activities.

The money laundering offense under Part 1of Article 218 of the CC (2014[5]), which constitutes the basic offense, is punishable by a fine of up to five thousand monthly calculation indicators (MCI) or by corrective labour of the same amount, or by restriction of freedom for a term not exceeding six years, or by imprisonment for the same term, with confiscation of property. Money laundering under Part 2 of Article 218 of the CC, including acts committed by a person utilizing their official position, is punishable by a fine ranging from three thousand to seven thousand MCIs or by corrective labour of the same amount, or by imprisonment for a term ranging from three to seven years, with confiscation of property. Money laundering under Part 3 of Article 218 of the CC, committed by a person authorised to perform public functions, or by a person equated with such, or by an official, or by a person holding a responsible government position, if connected with the misuse of their official position, is punishable by imprisonment for a term ranging from five to ten years, with confiscation of property, and in cases specified in Clause 1, incurs a lifelong prohibition from holding certain positions or engaging in specific activities.

Additionally, pursuant to Para 6 of the Regulatory Resolution of the Supreme Court of the Republic of Kazakhstan (2015[14]), if the sanction of the article under which an individual is found guilty provides for alternative types of punishment, courts are required to consider the possibility of imposing the most lenient of these penalties.

5.3 Effectiveness, proportionality and dissuasiveness of sanctions

According to Article 30(1) of the UNCAC (United Nations, 2004[3]), each State Party is obligated to ensure the application of criminal sanctions for the commission of any crime recognised as such under this Convention, which take into account the severity of the offense. As stated in Article 30(3) of the Convention, each State Party seeks to ensure that the discretionary legal powers provided in its legislation regarding the prosecution of individuals for [corruption] offenses are utilised to achieve maximum effectiveness in law enforcement measures against them, while duly considering the necessity to prevent the commission of such crimes in the future. Furthermore, Article 30(5) of the Convention stipulates that each State Party considers the degree of severity of the relevant offenses when deliberating the possibility of early or conditional release of individuals convicted of such crimes. Additionally, Article 30(7) of the Convention (United Nations, 2004[3]) states that when justified by the severity of the offense, each State Party considers the possibility of establishing procedures to deprive, for a specified period established in its domestic legislation, by court decision or by any other appropriate means, individuals convicted of crimes recognised under this Convention of the right: (a) to hold public office; and (b) to hold a position in any enterprise that is wholly or partially owned by the state.

The Criminal Law Convention on Corruption of adopted by the Council of Europe (1999[17]), which is not legally binding for Kazakhstan but serves as an example of best practices, contains even more detailed provisions regarding sanctions for corruption offenses. According to Article 19 of this Convention, considering the seriousness of the criminal offenses classified as such under the Convention, each Party provides for effective, proportionate, and dissuasive sanctions and measures regarding these offenses, including, if committed by natural persons, penalties involving deprivation of liberty, which may result in extradition. Each Party ensures that effective, proportionate, and dissuasive criminal or non-criminal sanctions, including financial penalties, are applied to legal entities held liable under Paras 1 and 2 of Article 18 of the Convention.

The official judicial statistics provided during this study indicate that, in 2021, a total of 892 individuals were convicted in criminal cases related to corruption offenses (within the classification of corruption offenses under the CC, which are significantly broader than that under UNCAC (United Nations, 2004[3])), 725 in 2022, and 916 in 2023. An analysis of the statistics on convictions for corruption offenses revealed that, between 2021 and 2023, the following number of individuals were convicted: for corrupt theft (Para 2 of Part 3 of Article 189 of the CC (2014[5])) - 59 individuals in 2021, 61 in 2022, and 81 in 2023; for abuse of official authority (Article 361 of the CC) - 78 individuals in 2021, 65 in 2022, and 57 in 2023; for passive bribery (Article 366 of the CC) - 214 individuals in 2021, 210 in 2022, and 222 in 2023; for active bribery (Article 367 of the CC) - 353 individuals in 2021, 192 in 2022, and 290 in 2023 (the highest number of convictions); for mediation in bribery (Article 368 of the CC) - 24 individuals in 2021, 20 in 2022, and 48 in 2023; and for laundering the proceeds of corruption - 1 individual in 2021. There were no such cases in 2022 and 2023. According to conviction statistics presented, the most common corruption offense is bribery, particularly active bribery of public officials. This may be explained by the fact that, in criminal cases involving active bribery, the perpetrators are predominantly private individuals. Moreover, such cases often involve instances where a public official (for example, a traffic police officer) refuses to accept a bribe and reports the offense. Additionally, many cases involve numerous bribe-givers — for example, drivers who offer bribes to customs or phytosanitary control officers.

The provided judicial statistics do not contain data on convictions for corruption in the private sector (Articles 250, 251, 253 of the CC (2014[5])). It is particularly noteworthy that there are virtually no convictions of public officials or affiliated individuals for the legalisation (laundering) of proceeds of corruption (only 1 conviction in 3 years).

The statistics on the types of penalties applied by national courts in corruption cases in 2021–2023 are presented in the table below.

Table 5.1. Statistics on imposed penalties for corruption offenses

Type of crime	Penalties imposed								
	Deprivation of liberty (total number of convicted persons)			Restriction of freedom			Penalty		
	2021	2022	2023	2021	2022	2023	2021	2022	2023
Embezzlement	16(59)	21(61)	32(81)	14	15	20	20	15	18
(Article 189 Part 3 Para 2, Article 189 Part 4 of the CC)	25(78)	20(65)	17(57)	45	28	28	4	1	9
Abuse of office (Art. 361 the CC)	74(214)	56(210)	63(222)	4	-	-	135	147	151
Receiving a bribe (Article 366 of the CC)	92(353)	52(192)	92(290)	15	6	7	244	91	183
Giving a bribe Article 367 of the CC	7(24)	2(20)	7(48)	1	-	-	16	15	30

Source: Data provided by Kazakhstan authorities

The statistics indicate that the percentage of imprisonment sentences imposed by courts for corruption offenses has consistently been less than 35%. Specifically, this includes embezzlement at 34%, abuse of office at 31%, passive bribery at 30%, active bribery at 28%, and mediation in bribery at 17%.

Moreover, the most common type of criminal penalty for all forms of bribery has been a multiple fine equivalent to the amount of the bribe. Judicial statistics also suggest that the most frequent prison sentences in cases of corruption offenses range widely from 1 to 10 years.

Of the 48 court verdicts on corruption offenses analysed for this study, 1 verdict resulted in an acquittal, while the other 47 resulted in convictions (some of which included partial acquittals regarding certain incriminated episodes).

The analysis of these sentences revealed the following:

For 2021, out of 11 convictions, 3 cases resulted in sentences of deprivation of liberty (ranging from 4 to 8 years, with actual serving), 8 cases resulted in sentences to fines, and in 1 case a sentence was restriction of liberty.

For 2022, among the 11 convictions, 4 cases imposed deprivation of liberty as a penalty (terms ranging from 1 to 10 years, with actual serving), while 7 cases were sentenced to fines.

For 2023, out of 25 convictions, in 11 cases sanctions were deprivation of liberty (terms ranging from 1.5 to 10 years; 1 case involved a deferred sentence, while the rest involved actual serving), in 12 cases fines were imposed, and 2 cases resulted in imposing restrictions of liberty.

From the 48 sentences analysed for the years 2021–2023, the following conclusions are possible:

- in cases of corruption offenses, the courts of Kazakhstan predominantly impose non-custodial sentences (mainly fines in multiples of the amount of the bribe).
- in cases where the court imposes an actual imprisonment on a public official for a corruption offense - the sentences predominantly look convincing (5-11 years of imprisonment), including in cases of high-level corruption (as a general rule),
- in none of the 48 analysed conviction sentences when imposing deprivation of liberty as a penalty was conditional conviction applied (since part 6 of Article 43 of the CC (2014[5]) does not allow conditional conviction in cases of corruption offenses, which should be noted as a positive approach), but one sentence was found with deferred execution of penalty (Article 74 of the CC, on the basis of the presence of a minor child of the convicted woman).

Box 5.1. Sanctions imposed for high-level corruption offenses

Below is the outline of sanctions in high-level corruption cases imposed from 2021 to 2023.

- The chairman of the state institution was convicted of embezzlement of KZT 6 527 956 994 (approximately USD 12 608 542) and sentenced for 8 years of imprisonment, with lifelong deprivation of the right to hold certain positions or engage in specific activities (case No. 7511-20-00-1/223).
- A Vice-Minister was convicted of abuse of office, causing damages worth KZT 40 638 265 000 (approximately USD 78 491 525). The damage was fully recovered before conviction. The Vice-Minister was sentenced for 7 years of imprisonment, with lifelong deprivation of the right to hold certain positions or engage in specific activities (case No. 7135-23-00-1/338).
- The Chairman of a judicial body of a regional court was convicted of receiving a bribe by extortion in the amount of KZT 19 000 000 (approximately USD 38 000), and sentenced for 9 years of imprisonment, with lifelong deprivation of the right to hold certain positions or engage in specific activities (case No. 3911-23-00-1/254).
- The following penalties were imposed based on a plea agreement: a deputy Head of a state institution was convicted of embezzlement for 5 years of imprisonment, with lifelong deprivation of the right to hold certain positions or engage in specific activities. The Head of the state institution convicted of complicity in embezzlement and money laundering for 6 years of imprisonment, with lifelong deprivation of the right to hold certain positions or engage in specific activities. The manager of the LLC was convicted of complicity in embezzlement and money laundering for 6 years of imprisonment, with lifelong deprivation of the right to hold certain positions or engage in specific activities. The value of embezzled property was KZT 14 565 318 010 (approximately USD 28 132 451), which was fully compensated during the investigation stage (case No. 7199-23-00-1a/210).
- A judge of the city court was convicted of receiving a bribe of KZT 2 000 000 (approximately USD 3 860) under aggravated circumstances and sentenced for 3 years of imprisonment, with lifelong deprivation of the right to hold certain positions or engage in specific activities (case No. 3140-23-00-1/76).

Note: Information is based on available court rulings issued in 2021–2023 and may not be exhaustive.

It appears that in the first four cases of high-level corruption, the amounts of imprisonment in general can be recognised as meeting the requirements of effectiveness, proportionality and ensuring a deterrent effect, while the last sentence (to the city judge) can hardly be recognised as meeting such standards. The penalty for passive bribery (bribe taking) under aggravating circumstances committed by a judge in the form of only 3 years of imprisonment (although real) does not look like an effective and proportionate criminal sanction, which would provide a sufficient deterrent effect, in particular, for other public officials, including judges.

The analysis of Kazakhstan's criminal legislation regarding criminal sanctions for corruption offenses, along with the practice of its application, leads to the conclusion that, despite significant legislative efforts aimed at aligning the laws with international standards, particularly in terms of ensuring effective, proportionate, and dissuasive penalties for corruption offenses, there remain areas for improvement both in the legislative framework and in law enforcement practices that require further enhancement.

OECD has already emphasised that high-level and complex corruption continues to be a key challenge in the Central Asian region, with most countries having made insufficient effort to adequately address it. The most common obstacles to effectively tackling high-level corruption in the region are the lack of genuine political will to investigate such offenses. Also of concern are the disproportionate and lenient sanctions that courts have applied in corruption cases (OECD, 2020[18]).

OECD has noted (2017[8]) that the CC (2014[5]), adopted in July 2014, revised the sanctions for corruption offenses. The main sanctions for corruption offenses remained unchanged. However, bribe taking and bribe giving by public officials and persons occupying responsible public positions were redesigned from qualified offenses to basic ones. This led to a reduction in the term of imprisonment as a possible sanction for such individuals.

In addition, other changes have been made to the sanctions for corruption offenses:

1) instead of a fine in a certain fixed amount (a certain number of monthly calculation indicators), a fine multiple of the amount of the bribe was introduced,

2) a fine multiple of the amount of the bribe is applied as an alternative sanction for all offenses of receiving or giving a bribe, whereas previously only imprisonment was applied for aggravated bribery

3) instead of depriving individuals of the right to hold certain positions or engage in specific activities for a specified term, mandatory lifelong deprivation of the right to hold certain positions or engage in specific activities has been introduced for all categories of corruption offenses. The CC prohibits the application of conditional sentencing, which was a positive innovation that had potential of contributing to the effectiveness of penalties for corruption offenses.

The amendments to certain provisions on prosecution for corruption offenses were welcomed, specifically the linking of the amount of the fine to the amount of the bribe, the mandatory lifetime ban on holding public service positions in case of prosecution for corruption, and the elimination of conditional exemption from liability in case of corruption offenses. These innovations were assessed as progressive and considered as best practices. However, there was concern about the shift in emphasis to financial sanctions instead of imprisonment for serious corruption offenses. Limiting sanctions for bribery offenses to financial compensation may not be sufficiently deterrent and may allow corrupt officials to avoid severe penalty by paying off (OECD, 2017[19]). This was also indicated by the increase in the number of fines compared to the application of imprisonment. In this regard, Kazakhstan was recommended to revise the sanctions for corruption offenses to ensure effectiveness and proportionality, including providing for mandatory imprisonment for serious corruption offenses; and to conduct an annual analysis of the imposed penalties for corruption offenses, assessing their effectiveness, and publishing the results of such analysis.

OECD has further noted (OECD, 2024[9]) that, according to information from NGOs, the analysis of corruption cases for 2023 revealed the following problematic aspects: courts increasingly imposed other sanctions but imprisonment. Most often, these were fines or restrictions of liberty for serious offenses. For example, of 10 randomly selected convictions for abuse of office (Article 361 of the CC (2014[5])) in 2023, 3 sentences included restrictions of liberty ranging from 3.6 to 4 years, without confiscation, and 7 sentences involved fines. Under Article 366 (Receiving a Bribe), out of 10 randomly selected cases, 8 resulted in fines, 1 in imprisonment, and 1 in restriction of liberty. Fines were imposed even for receiving bribes of substantial amounts (KZT 1.5 million and more).

Nevertheless, three sentences issued in 2023 against three vice ministers for corruption offenses resulted in penalties of imprisonment. It aligned with the penalties imposed in 5 high-level corruption cases from 2021 to 2025, specifically, imprisonment without conditional or other forms of release.

Yet not all sanctions for corruption offenses in the current the CC (2014[5]) can be regarded as sufficiently effective, proportionate and dissuasive as required by international standards.

For example, abuse of office (Article 361 of the CC (2014[5])) entails various penalties under Part 1 (as the main corpus delicti), ranging from a fine of up to 2 000 MCI (as of 1 January 2024, approximately USD 14 000), including alternatively correctional work, or community service, or restriction of freedom for up to 2 years, to imprisonment for the same term. The same act committed by a law enforcement officer (Part 2 of Article 361 of the CC) is sanctioned with the same wide range of penalties, ranging from a fine of up to 4 000 MCI (approximately USD 28 000) to imprisonment for up to 4 years. The same act committed by a person holding a responsible public position (Part 3 of Article 361 of the CC) is punishable by the same wide range of penalties, from a fine of up to 5 000 MCI (approximately USD 35 000) to imprisonment for up to 5 years.

Due to the stipulated sanctions, the offense specified in Part 1 of Article 361 of the CC (2014[5]) falls under the category of minor offenses, while the acts outlined in parts 2 and 3 of Article 361 of the CC are categorised as medium offenses (according to the categorisation in Article 11 of the CC). This allows them to be eligible for different types of mitigation of liability, penalties, or serving of sentences (for example, the application of Part 1 of Article 55 of the CC, which allows for non-imposition of imprisonment as a penalty in cases of voluntary compensation for damages and redress for harm caused by minor or medium offenses, etc.).

It should also be noted that provision of a fine as an alternative penalty for abuse of office committed by a person holding a responsible public position raises concerns regarding the effectiveness of sanctions for such high-level corruption.

Similar questions arise in the context of certain provisions of Article 189 of the CC (2014[5]) (embezzlement). For example, when committed by a person using their official position (Part 2), embezzlement is sanctioned for alternative penalties such as a fine of up to three thousand MCI (approximately USD 21 000), corrective labour, community service, restriction of liberty for up to 4 years, or imprisonment for the same term, classifying the act as a medium offense and qualifying it for the potential application of legal mitigations from the listed penalties.

Furthermore, when committed by a person authorised to perform governmental functions, or equivalent, or by an official, or a person holding a responsible state position, if committed in conjunction with the use of their official position, the embezzlement is sanctioned with a fine of ten to twenty times the value of the stolen property or imprisonment for a term of 2 to 7 years. Therefore, in cases of serious high-level corruption (embezzlement under aggravating circumstances), such a high-ranking offender has the alternative option of receiving a fine (albeit a significant one) while still avoiding actual imprisonment.

Similar issues arise regarding penalties for bribery offenses (receiving and giving bribes, Articles 366 and 367 of the CC (2014[5])). The basic offenses of both giving and receiving bribes, due to the prescribed penalties (a maximum of up to 5 years of imprisonment), are classified as medium offenses, regardless of the position of the individual committing them (exceptions include passive bribery committed by law enforcement personnel, individuals holding a responsible state position in law enforcement, or judges, as outlined in part 1-1 of Article 366 of the CC).

The giving or receiving a bribe by an individual holding a responsible state position (apart from the exceptions noted in Part 1-1 of Article 366 of the CC (2014[5])) is not considered an aggravating factor in these offenses. Thus, if a minister or official of that level receives a bribe of an insignificant amount, it would be classified as a medium offense with all the associated legal consequences.

Moreover, for any type of bribery offense (active or passive), as well as for mediation in bribery (whether it is a basic, qualified, or especially qualified offense where applicable), there is always the possibility of imposing one of two alternative types of penalties (imprisonment or a fine equivalent to a multiple of the bribe amount). And despite the impressive ranges of multiples of the bribe amount set as alternative penalties (from twenty times to eighty times the amount of the bribe), this does not enhance the effectiveness of such sanctions, especially in cases involving systemic bribery (for example, a customs officer caught with the daily earnings from 25 drivers amounting to a total of USD 500) or in high-level corruption cases, where a high-ranking official could easily pay a large fine from their overall wealth, the legitimacy of which may raise reasonable questions, merely to avoid imprisonment.

The ability to pay a fine, even a substantial one, instead of being sanctioned with imprisonment does not appear to be an effective, proportionate, or convincing sanction that provides a sufficient deterrent effect, particularly in high-level corruption cases.

The penalty for the aggravated bribery intermediation (Part 2 of Article 368 of the CC (2014[5])), including when committed by an individual using his official position), an alternative penalty in the form of a multiple fine or imprisonment for up to 6 years does not appear convincing enough for cases when the intermediaries are high-level officials, or the amounts of bribes are significant.

An additional issue to ensure the cogency of penalty for active and passive bribery is Article 56 of the CC, which provides for lesser sanctions (term or amount of penalty) for preparation for a crime (cannot exceed a half of the maximum term or amount of the principal type of penalty provided for the relevant completed crime) or attempted crime (cannot exceed 3/4 of the maximum term or amount of the principal type of penalty for the relevant completed crime). The problem arises due to the fact that Kazakhstan has not yet criminalised the offer and promise of a bribe[9], as well as the acceptance of an offer or promise of a bribe as a completed offense, which is a recognised international standard, for example, Article 15 of the UNCAC (United Nations, 2004[3]), Articles 2 and 3 of the Council of Europe Criminal Law Convention on Corruption (1999[17]), Article 1 of the OECD Convention on Combatting Bribery of Foreign Public Officials in International Business Transactions (OECD, 1997[20]). Therefore, before the above elements of bribery are criminalised as a completed offense, it is recommended, as an interim measure, to remove corruption offenses—particularly all bribery offenses—from the scope of Article 56 of the CC (2014[5]).

Crimes of corruption in the private sector (Articles 250, 251, 253 of the CC (2014[5])) have similar shortcomings as described above in the context of crimes of corruption in the public sector.

Thus, it is recommended to revise the sanctions for corruption offenses in order to ensure the effectiveness, proportionality and proper deterrent effect of such sanctions.

In turn, practical application of fines that are multiples of the amount of the bribe or other corrupt benefits is a positive and progressive practice.

Analysis of official judicial statistics of convictions for corruption offenses in 2021–2023 illustrates that the most common type of penalty for corruption offenses in practice (primarily for active and passive bribery) is a fine. For example, 1 012 persons were convicted with a fine only for bribery in 2021–2023 (out of a total of 1 573 individuals convicted for this type of corruption offenses), which is about 65%.

Among the 47 convictions for corruption offenses analysed in this study for the years 2021–2023, fines were imposed as the primary penalty in 27 cases (57%). The examination of the verdicts revealed that courts determine the deadlines for the payment of fines at their discretion, and there are no clear criteria upon which this determination is based. Verdicts with payment deadlines of 15 and 30 days, 1, 2, 3, and 6 months were found, as well as a verdict without a specified payment deadline (Case No. 3511-22-00-1/158). The CC (2014[5]) in Part 4 of Article 41 only stipulates that the deadline for paying a fine is calculated from the moment the verdict becomes final and cannot exceed three years as per the court's ruling. It seems appropriate for the Supreme Court to develop criteria for determining payment deadlines for fines as a penalty based on the law and judicial practice to limit the current judicial discretion in this area to reasonable bounds.

The attachment of the amount of the fine in the criminal law to the amount of the bribe and other types of illicit benefits, using a multiplicative approach to determine fines as penalties for corruption offenses, can generally be regarded as a positive practice (for example, bribery under Part 1 of Article 367 of the CC (2014[5]) can be punished with a fine of 20 to 30 times the amount of the bribe). However, in the CC, the multiplicative fine is stipulated as a primary punishment for corruption offenses, rather than as an additional penalty to imprisonment, restriction of liberty, or other sanctions, even in cases of serious and especially serious corruption offenses.

Thus, in practice, there is a trend towards shifting the focus to financial sanctions (multiplicative fines or fixed fines) instead of applying imprisonment as a primary penalty in every case of serious corruption offenses (such as bribery, embezzlement, and abuse of office). This shift raises concerns about the alignment of such practices with the goals of effectiveness, proportionality, and adequate deterrent effect of the imposed sanctions. As previously noted, limiting sanctions for bribery offenses to financial compensation may not provide sufficient deterrence and may allow corrupt officials to evade strict punishment by paying a fine (OECD, 2017[19]). Below are several examples of typical verdicts from the 48 analysed that illustrate the problematic approaches to imposing penalties in the form of multiplicative fines as applied in practice.

Thus, by the verdict in case № 1956-21-00-1/15 a customs inspector was convicted for 24 episodes of taking bribes totalling KZT 24,000 (about USD 48) to a multiple fine of KZT 1 680 000 (USD 3 400). It appears that such a sentence will hardly have a sufficient deterrent effect on other customs officers prone to systematic bribes. The same sentence sentenced 24 drivers (bribe-takers) to a fine of KZT 10,000 each and were released from this penalty under an amnesty.

By the verdict in case № 3310-23-00-1/197 the Head of Department of the Ministry of Health Protection was sentenced under Part 3 Article 366 of the CC to a fine of KZT 3 850 000 (about USD 7 800) for taking a bribe of KZT 110 000 (USD 220) for issuing a licence for medical services. Given the relatively high level of the convicted person's position and the high corruption risks inherent in this position (given the importance of the licences issued), such a sanction does not look sufficiently effective and convincing either.

Considering the results of the analysis, it is recommended to reconsider the existing approaches to applying multiples of fines to the amount of a bribe or other corrupt benefit as the main alternative sanction for serious corruption and to consider that all serious and especially serious corruption offenses should carry a non-alternative sanction of imprisonment for appropriate periods of time sufficient to ensure effectiveness, proportionality and appropriate deterrent effect. Fines (multiples of the amount of the bribe or other form of corrupt benefit, or fines of a certain amount) could be an additional penalty for corruption offenses, rather than the main penalty for them.

Practical application of deprivation of liberty for corruption offenses

During 2021–2023 courts predominantly imposed imprisonment in high-level corruption cases. All five such cases resulted in actual prison sentences, although one conviction appeared insufficiently convincing. Overall, this can be noted as a good practice. In low- and middle-level corruption cases, the primary penalty was a fine, as outlined above.

As a positive practice regarding the application of imprisonment for corruption offenses in Kazakhstan, it should also be noted that the CC (2014[5]) generally excludes the use of suspended sentences for such offenses (Part 6 of Article 63 of the CC).

Nevertheless, it appears, based on the analysis of the available case-law, that the main issue affecting the effectiveness of imprisonment as a sanction for corruption offenses is that (1) legal provisions still allow options to avoid actual imprisonment in cases where such a penalty would otherwise be effective, proportionate and persuasive; and (2) even in cases where courts impose a penalty in the form of real imprisonment for serious corruption offenses, it is essentially possible for a defendant to be released after a relatively short period of time. This does not ensure the preventive effect of such penalty. In addition, such a practice may undermine public confidence in the criminal justice system. Both of these issues are further analysed below.

According to Para 1 of Part 1 of Article 55 of the CC (2014[5]), if the article or part of the article of the Special Part of the CC, under which a person is found guilty, provides for a less strict, than imprisonment, basic penalty, imprisonment shall not be imposed for crimes of minor or medium gravity, if the person has voluntarily compensated for property damage, amended for moral and other harm caused by the offense. At the same time, some corruption offenses belong precisely to the category of crimes of minor or medium gravity.

In addition, Parts 4 and 5 of Article 55 of the CC (2014[5]) also provide that in the presence of exceptional circumstances related to the goals and motives of the act, the role of the perpetrator, his behaviour during or after the commission of an offense and other circumstances that significantly reduce the degree of public danger of the act, as well as subject to the active assistance of a participant in the group criminal offense to disclose the acts committed by the group, the penalty may be imposed below the lowest limit provided for by the relevant article of the Special Part of the CC, or the court may impose a penalty of less than the lowest limit provided for by the relevant article of the Special Part of the CC. Both individual mitigating circumstances and the totality of such circumstances may be recognised as exceptional. Provisions of the Article 55 of the CC are not applicable to offenses listed in Part 8 of Article 55 of the CC, which do not include corruption offenses. That potentially makes it possible to level out strict custodial sentences for corruption offenses at the stage of determining the penalty. In view of the previously mentioned international standards, it is recommended to exclude corruption offenses from the scope of Part 1 of Article 55 of the CC and exclude them from the scope of Part 4 of Article 55 of the CC, supplementing the exceptions in Part 8 of Article 55 of the CC with an explicit reference to corruption offenses.

In addition, a convict may benefit from replacement of the unexecuted part of penalty by a more lenient kind of penalty or reduction of the term of the imposed punishment under Article 73 of the CC (2014[5]). According to this provision, to the person serving imprisonment for offenses of little or medium gravity or serious offenses, in case of full compensation of damage caused by an offense, or absence of malicious violations of the order of serving the sentence, the remaining unexecuted part of the sentence can be replaced by the court with a milder kind of penalty. Thus, the person can be completely or partially released from serving an additional kind of penalty, except for penalties appointed for life.

The unserved portion of the penalty may be replaced with a milder penalty after a convict has served at least one-quarter of the sentence for committing an offense of minor or medium gravity or one-third of the sentence for serious offenses, as specified in Parts 1 and 2 of Article 73 of the CC (2014[5]). Additionally, Part 4 of Article 73 of the CC allows for the reduction of up to half of the unserved sentence for individuals serving imprisonment for any type of crime, including serious and very serious offenses. This is contingent upon the person having contributed to the disclosure and investigation of crimes committed by a criminal group or having fulfilled all the conditions of a procedural agreement during the period of serving their sentence. This provision also does not specify corruption offenses as an exception to the application of this rule. It is recommended that such exceptions be expanded to include corruption offenses by adding them to both lists of exceptions in Part 1 and Part 4 of Article 73 of the CC.

The provisions regarding conditional early release from sentence should also be considered in this context. According to Part 1 of Article 72 of the CC (2014[5]), a person serving a sentence of restriction of freedom or imprisonment can be granted conditional early release after serving the terms specified in Parts 3 and 4, and 5 of this article, if the court determines that complete execution of the sentence is not necessary to achieve rehabilitation. The same category of persons is also eligible for conditional parole, provided they have fully compensated for the damage caused by the crime and have not committed serious violations of the sentence enforcement order.

Part 1 of Article 72 of the CC (2014[5]) also permits the court to grant parole to certain categories of offenders after they have served the periods specified in parts 3 and 5 of this article. These categories include pregnant women, women with young children, men raising young children alone, women aged 58 and over, men aged 63 and over, and persons with Group I or II disabilities who are serving imprisonment sentences for serious or especially serious offenses, including corruption offenses.

Additionally, a person serving imprisonment for a serious or especially serious corruption offense may be eligible for parole if they have fulfilled all the conditions of a procedural agreement on co-operation, and after serving the periods outlined in Parts 3 and 5 of Article 72 of the CC (2014[5]).

In this case, a person may be fully or partially released from serving an additional penalty. Although this provision includes specific rules for its application to certain types of corruption offenses under certain conditions, there is a risk that general parole rules for serving sentences could be applied independently to corruption offenses in practice. This could lead to unjustified leniency, including in cases of high-level corruption. Therefore, it is recommended to exclude corruption offenses from the scope of Article 72 of the CC (2014[5]) altogether or to restrict its application to corruption offenses to exceptional cases that are clearly and explicitly defined.

During the interviews conducted for this study, especially among non-governmental stakeholders, respondents confirmed that in Kazakhstan there are practical problems caused by legislative flaws and gaps. These issues, particularly during sentencing and, more often, during sentence execution, enable individuals convicted of corruption offenses to avoid imprisonment or proper enforcement of their sentences. Consequently, this undermines the effectiveness of existing penalties for corruption offenses as provided by law.

Similar data were obtained during the baseline monitoring of anti-corruption reforms in Kazakhstan (OECD, 2024[9]). According to non-governmental sector, in practice, parole is often granted in Kazakhstan for serious and especially serious corruption offenses. For example, one of the influential relatives of a former state leader was sentenced in September 2023 to six years of imprisonment for embezzling KZT 14 billion from a state-owned company. By 6 November 2023, he was already reportedly released. This early release was due to the return of illegally acquired assets and replacing the unserved portion of his sentence with a suspended sentence. However, journalists later revealed that the "return of assets" did not actually occur (2025[13]).

Application of dismissal from office

The analysis of verdicts revealed that in every case where defendants were found guilty of any corruption offense, they were consistently sentenced to an additional penalty of life (indefinite) deprivation of the right to hold specific positions or engage in particular activities, without exception.

This is confirmed by the findings in the Baseline Report of the Fifth Round of Monitoring of Anti-Corruption Reforms in Kazakhstan (OECD, 2024[9]), which established that, in 2023, all public officials found guilty of corruption offenses were dismissed from their offices (OECD, 2024[9]).

In this regard, it is important to highlight the provisions of Part 2 of Article 50 of the CC (2014[5]), which establish that, for committing corruption offenses, deprivation of the right to hold specific positions or engage in certain activities is mandatory. This includes a lifetime ban on holding positions in civil service, judiciary, local self-government bodies, the National Bank of Kazakhstan and its agencies, the authorised body on regulation, control and supervision of the financial market and financial organisations, state organisations and subjects of the state sector. Thus, subjects of quasi-state sector are state enterprises, limited liability partnerships, joint stock companies, including national management holdings, national holdings, national companies, the participant or shareholder of which is the state, as well as subsidiaries, affiliates and other legal entities affiliated with them in accordance with legislative acts of Kazakhstan (Article 3 of the Budget Code) (2008[21]).

Such legislative regulation, as well as the application of these provisions in practice by prosecutors and courts, should be noted as an example of a best practice approach to this issue in the region.

Liability of legal persons for corruption offenses

In accordance with article 26 of the UNCAC (United Nations, 2004[3]), each State Party shall adopt such measures as may be necessary, considering its legal principles, to establish the liability of legal persons for participation in the offenses set forth in the Convention. Subject to the legal principles of the State Party, the liability of legal persons may be criminal, civil or administrative. The imposition of liability of legal persons shall not prejudice the criminal liability of natural persons who have committed the offenses in question. Each State Party shall ensure that legal persons held liable in accordance with this article are subject to effective, proportionate and dissuasive criminal or non-criminal sanctions, including monetary sanctions.

Practice shows that corruption offenses, in particular high-level corruption, are often committed in the interests or for the benefit of legal persons, especially when substantial corrupt proceeds (benefits) are involved. However, the complex corporate structures and collective decision-making processes of large corporate structures often make the detection and prosecution of such acts of corruption much more difficult. Often the ultimate beneficial owners of companies, the real perpetrators and initiators of complex corporate criminal schemes find ways to cover themselves with the so-called corporate veil and avoid responsibility. In such cases, the individual liability of corporate agents, rank and file or even more senior corporate officers will not have an adequate deterrent effect on the corporation and its owner(s), who may in the future reap the benefits that the commission of a corruption offense has brought to them and their company. In many such cases, only an effective model of corporate responsibility for corruption, with substantial sanctions, including financial penalties, can ensure that sanctions for serious corruption offenses are truly credible, i.e., effective and dissuasive.

For this reason, Kazakhstan has been repeatedly recommended in the past by various international organisations to introduce into its legislation and practice an effective model of corporate liability of legal entities for criminal offenses of corruption.

For example, GRECO explicitly recommended Kazakhstan to "take necessary legislative measures to establish adequate liability of legal entities for corruption offenses and to provide effective, proportionate and convincing sanctions in this part", having previously analysed and recognised the existing model of liability of companies in Kazakhstan based on the Code of Administrative Offenses and the practice of its application as irrelevant and ineffective (2022[11]).

This recommendation was also made by the OECD within the monitoring under the framework of the IAP. Thus, the Report of the 4th Round of Monitoring of Kazakhstan under IAP (OECD, 2017[8]) noted that the relevant recommendation of the previous (3rd round) monitoring was not implemented by Kazakhstan, accordingly, the Report formulated a new recommendation #19: to establish effective and efficient liability of legal entities for corruption offenses with proportional sanctions that will be commensurate with the crime committed, in accordance with international standards and best practices.

Finally, the Baseline Report of the Fifth Round of Monitoring of Anti-Corruption Reforms in Kazakhstan (OECD, 2024[9]) confirmed that there were no liability of legal persons for corruption offenses in Kazakhstan (only administrative liability). The existing provisions of the Code on Administrative Offenses of Kazakhstan (2014[22]) were analysed in previous rounds of the OECD Istanbul Action Plan assessment of Kazakhstan and were found to be ineffective and insufficient (OECD, 2024[9]).

Thus, it remains only to recommend once again to the country to introduce an effective mechanism of liability of legal entities for corruption offenses, based on both international standards and best practices of the countries of the region. All arguments in favour of such a need have already been repeatedly presented in the above-mentioned and other reports of international organisations and are not duplicated in this study.

Statistics on penalties for corruption offenses

The current official judicial statistics on sanctions imposed by courts in cases of corruption offenses and laundering of proceeds thereof could be more informative if they comprised data on the types of sanctions imposed on different categories of officials (i.e., disaggregated by the level and type of officials sanctioned). It is recommended that the official statistics be further developed so that such data can be included in the future.

5.4 Statute of limitations and immunities against prosecution

Statute of limitations for corruption offenses

The UNCAC (United Nations, 2004[3]) provides in article 29 that each State Party shall, where appropriate, establish under its domestic law a long statute of limitations period for the commencement of proceedings in respect of any offenses established in accordance with that Convention and shall establish a longer statute of limitations period or the possibility of suspending the running of the statute of limitations period in cases where a person suspected of having committed an offense has evaded the administration of justice.

According to Article 71 of the CC (2014[5]), a person shall be exempted from criminal liability if the following terms [general rule] have expired from the date of committing a criminal offense: 10 years after the commission of a serious offense, a corruption offense of minor or medium gravity, and 15 years after the commission of a particularly serious offense.

The statute of limitations shall be calculated from the date of commission of the criminal offense and until the court sentence enters into legal force (Paras 1 and 2 of Article 71 of the CC (2014[5])). In addition, in accordance with Part 4 of Article 71 of the CC, the statute of limitations shall be suspended if the person who committed the offense evades investigation or trial. In this case, the statute of limitations shall be resumed from the moment of apprehension of the person or his or her confession. At the same time, a person may not be held criminally liable if, since the commission of the crime, the statute of limitations has not been interrupted and the following time limits have expired: 15 years after commission of a serious crime, a corruption offense of minor and medium gravity, and 20 years after commission of a particularly serious crime.

The running of the statute of limitations shall be interrupted if, before the expiration of the time limits specified in Para 1 of Article 71 of the CC (2014[5]), the person who committed a serious or especially serious crime commits a new serious or especially serious crime. In such cases, the calculation of the statute of limitations shall begin anew from the date of commission of the new crime. In other cases, if before the expiration of the statute of limitations the person commits a crime again, the statute of limitations for each crime shall run independently. In accordance with Para 4-1 of this article, the statute of limitations shall be suspended from the moment of receipt by the court or criminal prosecution body of a motion to conclude a procedural agreement on confession of guilt and return of illegally acquired assets from a suspect, accused, defendant or his defence counsel until the moment of its full execution. If one of the parties refuses to conclude a procedural agreement on plea bargain and return of illegally acquired assets, the statute of limitations shall be resumed. At the same time, Part 6 of Article 71 of the CC (2014[5]) provides for crimes, when, by way of exception, statutes of limitations are not applied to persons who committed them. This list in the current wording of the article does not include corruption crimes or certain types thereof and legalisation (laundering) of proceeds of crime, including from corruption.

Analysis of the norms of the current criminal legislation of Kazakhstan in terms of statutes of limitation allows to conclude that the increased statutes of limitation established by law for corruption offenses of minor and medium gravity (10 years as a general rule and 15 years in case of evasion of investigation or trial) are certainly a positive practice (although the same statute of limitation of 10 years for ordinary cases and 15 years for cases of evasion - as for serious corruption offenses - looks insufficiently progressive in terms of the statute of limitation for corruption offenses). At the same time, it should be borne in mind that until 12 July 2018, Part 6 of Article 71 of the CC (2014[5]) included corruption offenses in the list of crimes to which statutes of limitations did not apply at all, which was considered by the OECD Anti-Corruption Network for Eastern Europe and Central Asia (ACN) as a best practice and was separately positively assessed in the Report of the Fourth Round of Monitoring of Anti-Corruption Reforms in Kazakhstan (OECD, 2017[8]). Therefore, the exclusion of corruption offenses from the list of crimes to which statutes of limitations do not apply should be considered as a step backwards in reforming this institution in Kazakhstan, and it would be advisable to return to the wording of Part 6 of Article 71 of the CC, which was in force before it was amended on 12 July 2018, as well as to consider adding legalisation (laundering) of proceeds of corruption offenses to the list of crimes to which statutes of limitations do not apply.

In addition, attention should also be paid to the approach in Part 2 of Article 71 of the CC (2014[5]), according to which the statute of limitations is calculated until the court judgment enters into legal force, which could potentially create problems in practice and lead to the expiration of the time limits, for example, in cases of several rounds of court proceedings. To prevent such potential problems, an alternative approach could be suggested - to provide for the suspension of the statute of limitations from a prior point in time (e.g., from the moment criminal proceedings are initiated against a person, or a person is suspected/accused, or the case is sent to court for indictment, etc.).

It should also be noted that the official criminal pre-trial and judicial statistics for 2021–2023, which were provided for the purposes of the study, do not allow identifying cases of termination of criminal proceedings at the investigative and judicial stages on this very ground (Para 4, Part 1 of Article 35 of CPC (2014[6]) – for the expiration of the statute of limitations for bringing to criminal responsibility), as they combine in the corresponding column a variety of grounds for the pre-trial stage (the number of criminal offenses for which criminal cases have been terminated based on Paras 3), 4), 9), 10), 11), and 12) of part 1 of Article 35 and Article 36 of CPC). This way of keeping statistics does not also make it possible to determine whether cases were terminated on this basis against public officials or other categories of persons. It is recommended that the approach to statistics be changed to ensure that such data can be obtained in the future.

For the purposes of this study, no decisions of investigation bodies or courts on the termination of criminal cases on corruption in 2021–2023 on the basis of Para 4, part 1, Article 35 of CPC (2014[6]) (due to the expiration of the statute of limitations) were provided, so it was not possible to draw conclusions about the practice of application of this norm on the basis of procedural decisions.

In 2023, according to the information provided by authorities, no criminal cases were terminated due to expiration of the statute of limitations (OECD, 2024[9]). This information was consistent with verdicts of 48 corruption cases analysed for this study, since they did not include data on cases against any of the defendants or their accomplices being closed on the grounds of expiration of statute of limitation.

Investigators, prosecutors and judges interviewed for the study did not see any challenges with the application of statutory statutes of limitations in corruption cases and could not recall any cases terminated due to the expiration of statutes of limitations in 2021–2023. Representatives of non-governmental stakeholders also did not see significant problems with the application of the statute of limitations in corruption cases and stated that cases were dismissed due to the expiration of the statute of limitations, but not frequently, and did not pose a systemic problem. Nevertheless, they could not recall any specific examples of corruption cases being dismissed due to the expiration of statutes of limitations during the period covered by the study.

Immunities of public officials against enforcement steps

Pursuant to article 30(2) of the UNCAC (United Nations, 2004[3]), each State Party shall take such measures as may be necessary to establish or ensure, in accordance with its legal system and constitutional principles, an appropriate balance between any immunities or jurisdictional privileges accorded to its public officials in connection with the performance of their functions and the ability, if necessary, to effectively investigate, prosecute and adjudicate in accordance with its legal system and constitutional principles. Thus, as can be seen from the relevant provision, the UNCAC allows for the existence of functional immunities only and not general immunities.

In Kazakhstan, the following persons have procedural immunity[10] against criminal procedural actions: the President and ex-President, members of Parliament, candidates for the Presidency and Parliament, the Chairman, Deputy Chairman, judge of the Constitutional Court, judges, the Prosecutor General and the Commissioner for Human Rights. At the same time, immunities are not limited to acts committed in connection with the performance of official duties (i.e. immunities are of a general rather than functional nature).

Detailed information on the legislative regulation of Kazakhstan with regard to the criteria and procedure for lifting immunities from the specified types of public officials and existing shortcomings of such regulation in terms of international standards is contained in the Report of the Fourth Round of Monitoring of Anti-Corruption Reforms in Kazakhstan (OECD, 2017[8]). The existence of challenges with clarity of grounds (criteria) for lifting immunities and detailed regulation by legislation of procedures for their removal in Kazakhstan was confirmed during the Baseline Report of the Fifth Round of Monitoring of Anti-Corruption Reforms in Kazakhstan (OECD, 2024[9]).

The main problems with legislative regulation of immunities in Kazakhstan can be summarised as follows:

- Immunities are general in nature and are non-functional (not tied to job-related actions).
- The range of public officials with immunities and the procedural limitations associated with immunities is too broad.
- There are no clear criteria in the law for the consent of the Prosecutor General of Kazakhstan to continue a pre-trial investigation or to refuse such a pre-trial investigation after the registration of a reason for the initiation of a pre-trial investigation (Article 547 of CPC (2014[6]) (in relation to a member of Parliament), Article 549 of CPC (judges of the Constitutional Court), Article 550 of CPC (judges), etc.).
- There are no clear criteria in the law for the decision to consent to the detention, custody, house arrest, bail or criminal prosecution of a judge by the President, based on the opinion of the Supreme Judicial Council, or by the Senate of the Parliament.
- Provisions of CPC (2014[6]) or other legislative acts do not regulate in detail the procedures for lifting immunities from criminal prosecution in respect of judges.

Para 10 Part 1 of Article 35 of CPC (2014[6]) provides a separate ground for termination of a criminal case (in connection with the refusal to consent to criminal prosecution of a person who has privileges or immunity from criminal prosecution). The legislation does not regulate the question of what can happen to such a criminal case further - whether it can be reopened or whether the decision to terminate the case can be reversed if the person loses his position (and with it the past immunity) or if the composition of the body that refused to lift immunity changes, etc. It seems that the legislation should be amended in such a way that it gives the possibility of reviewing a decision to terminate a criminal case in connection with a refusal to lift immunity if the relevant circumstances change.

In addition, it seems that this issue is not clearly regulated by the legislator, but immunity in Kazakhstan extends in practice to acts committed prior to assuming a position entitling to immunity. This was confirmed by practitioners during the interviews. This problem will be eliminated with the transition from general immunities to functional immunities, which the country is recommended to do as a matter of priority.

Also, the current legislation of the country does not give a clear answer to the question of whether it is possible to reapply for the lifting of immunity in case of an initial refusal (for example, on the basis of new arguments or in connection with new evidence) and practically staff - investigators and prosecutors during interviews with them could not give an unambiguous answer to this question either, rather leaning towards the idea that it would be impossible to reapply. It would be advisable to clearly regulate such a possibility and clear grounds for its application in the law. In addition, national legislation did not contain any provisions that would suspend the statute of limitations for criminal liability for corruption if immunity was waived. If there was a norm on non-application of statutes of limitations to cases of such category (as it was before 12 July 2018), this would not be an issue. However, in the absence of this rule, it would be advisable to provide in the law for such a ground for suspending the statute of limitations for criminal liability.

It should also be noted that statistics on applications to lift immunity and the results of their consideration are not publicly available, and at the national level statistics on refusals to lift immunity and statistics on the termination of criminal cases separately on the basis of Para 10 Part 1 of Article 35 of CPC are not kept. The absence of such statistics makes it impossible to assess the extent to which immunities of high-ranking officials from prosecution for corruption-related offenses function in practice and to draw full conclusions about the practice of its application and the extent to which they hinder the investigation and prosecution of corruption offenses. It is therefore recommended that approaches to the maintenance of such statistics be improved.

With regard to the issues of application of the institution of immunities in practice, during the interviews with investigators, prosecutors and judges conducted as part of this study it became clear that the latter do not see the existing immunities as any obstacles in their practical work. One part of practitioners noted that there were no refusals to lift immunities in 2021–2023 at all. Another part reasonably noted that cases of refusal are not public, so even if there were such cases in 2021–2023, they would hardly be publicly known. Representatives of non-governmental stakeholders considered the general nature of immunities and the overly broad range of persons enjoying immunities to be a problem.

Out of verdicts analysed for this study, only two of them concerned individuals enjoying immunities, in particular judges (both verdicts were issued in 2023). The analysis of these two sentences showed that they lacked any data on the procedure for lifting immunities from defendants, including any impediments to proceedings it may have caused.

The Anti-Corruption Agency provided information that 22 persons with privileges from prosecution were convicted of a criminal offense between 2019 and 2024 (6 in 2019, 5 in 2020 and 2021, 1 in 2022, 3 in 2023 and 2 in 2024). All of them were judges. At the same time, the consent of the President (Article 79 of the Constitution of Kazakhstan (1995[23])) was not required for bringing to criminal responsibility for any of them, since the committed crimes were classified as serious and especially serious crimes. According to the data of the Agency for Combatting Corruption of Kazakhstan, in its practice during 2021–2023, there were no facts of refusal to lift immunities, and criminal cases were not terminated on such grounds.

Thus, the continuation of the pre-trial investigation in these cases was considered by the Prosecutor General and, according to the information provided, the necessary procedural consent was granted without delay.

In the process of conducting this study, there was no evidence that the procedures for lifting privileges and immunities would pose challenges to the investigation and prosecution of corruption offenses in Kazakhstan.

Database of Court Sentences

The current database of court decisions in Kazakhstan is a very restrictive tool in the context of searching for case law for research purposes. In particular, it does not allow searching for court decisions based on elementary search criteria (such as categories of offenses or articles of the CC under which sentences were issued) or keywords (confiscation, corruption, etc.) or the period of the judgment (e.g., for 2021–2023). In order to find a particular sentence in this database, it is necessary to enter the name of the convicted person, the exact date of the sentence and the exact name of the court that passed the sentence, which makes the search for judicial practice for the purposes of its generalization and research from the outside extremely problematic and difficult.

In this regard, it is recommended to significantly improve the public part of the database of court verdicts of Kazakhstan in order to make it possible to search for verdicts and other decisions on criminal cases on the basis of the above and other relevant search criteria.

Recommendations

- Ensure, through effective, proportionate and dissuasive criminal sanctions, that high-level corruption offenses (in terms of the level of the public official's position and/or the size of the corrupt benefit) are always categorised as serious or particularly serious offenses, including corruption in the private sector (under the criteria of the size of the corrupt benefit).
- Establish an aggravated form of bribery (active and passive) in the CC when this is committed by a person holding a responsible public position.
- Ensure that all serious and especially serious corruption offenses, particularly high-level corruption, are subject to custodial sentences of imprisonment that are non-optional, with durations sufficient to ensure their effectiveness, proportionality, and deterrent impact. Fines (multiples of the amount of the bribe or other form of corrupt benefit, or fines in a certain amount) may be an additional penalty (in addition to non-alternative sanctions of imprisonment) for serious and especially serious corruption offenses rather than an alternative to them. Fines could also be an additional penalty for other types of corruption offenses (of minor or medium) rather than the principal penalty for them.
- Exclude all corruption offenses from the scope of Part 2 and Part 3 of Article 56 of the CC (2014[5]) (imposing punishment for an incomplete crime). Exclude all bribery offenses from the scope of Part 2 and 3 of Article 56 of the CC or criminalise the offer and promise of a bribe, as well as the acceptance of an offer or promise of a bribe as a completed offense (for bribery in both the public and private sectors).
- Exclude corruption offenses from the scope of Part 1 of Article 55 of the CC (2014[5]) (imposition of a more lenient punishment than is provided for this criminal offense) and the scope of Part 4 of Article 55 of the CC, supplementing the exceptions in Part 8 of Article 55 of the CC with a reference to corruption offenses.
- Exclude corruption offenses from the scope of Article 72 of the CC (2014[5]) of Kazakhstan (parole from serving a sentence) or further limit the scope of its application to such offenses to exceptional cases that are clearly and unambiguously formulated.
- Exclude corruption offenses from the scope of Article 73 of the CC (2014[5]) (substitution of the unexecuted part of the sentence with a more lenient type of punishment or a reduction of the sentence).

- Introduce the liability of legal entities for corruption offenses in legislation based on international standards and best practices in the region, establishing effective, proportionate and dissuasive criminal sanctions for such legal entities, including financial sanctions.
- Ensure that judicial statistics on corruption offenses include data on the types of penalties imposed by courts on different categories of officials (i.e., a breakdown by level and type of official on whom certain penalties are imposed).
- Consider re-including corruption offenses in the list of crimes specified in Part 6 of Article 71 of the CC (2014[5]), to which the statute of limitations on criminal liability does not apply. Additionally, consider adding the offense of legalisation (laundering) of proceeds from corruption. Alternatively, consider expanding the grounds for suspending the statute of limitations in criminal cases by establishing that suspension applies at any stage of the proceedings prior to the entry into legal force of the judgment. This could include periods from the initiation of criminal proceedings, the suspicion or accusation of a suspect, or the referral of the case to court for indictment, among others.
- Ensure that official statistics clearly identify the number of persons whose criminal cases were terminated on the basis of Para 4 of Part 1 of Article 35 of CPC (2014[6]) (due to the expiration of the statute of limitations for bringing to criminal responsibility), and the number of those who belonged to the category of public officials.
- Ensure implementation of the recommendations of the Report of the Fourth Round of Monitoring under the IAP (OECD, 2017[8]) and address the shortcomings noted in the Baseline Report of the Fifth Round of Monitoring of Anti-Corruption Reforms in Kazakhstan under the IAP (OECD, 2024[9]) regarding immunities, in particular, ensure that general immunities are replaced by functional immunities, substantially reduce the number of public officials with immunities and procedural limitations on immunities.
- Consider amending legislation to permit review of decisions to terminate criminal cases due to refusal to lift immunity when relevant circumstances change, such as the loss of immunity entitlement or changes in the body authorised to lift immunity. Additionally, allow for submitting a repeated application to lift immunity based on new arguments or evidence. Lastly, include provisions to suspend the statute of limitations during these review processes to ensure timely prosecution.
- Ensure that official statistics include data on the number of applications to lift immunity from public officials and the outcomes of their consideration. Additionally, record the number of criminal case terminations under Para 10 of Part 1 of Article 35 of the CPC (2014[6]), with a breakdown by level and type of officials, and make this information publicly accessible.
- Enhance the public segment of the court verdicts database to enable searches for verdicts and other court decisions in criminal cases based on various criteria. These criteria may include crime categories, articles of the CC (2014[5]), keywords, the date of the ruling, and other relevant parameters.

References

Council of Europe (1999), *Criminal Law Convention on Corruption.* [17]

European Union (2024), *Directive (EU) 2024/1260 of the European Parliament and of the Council of 24 April 2024 on asset recovery and confiscation*, http://data.europa.eu/eli/dir/2024/1226/oj. [7]

European Union (2023), *STUDY EPRS | European Parliamentary Research Service Cost of Non-Europe Report.* [1]

European Union (2014), *Directive 2014/42/EU of the European Parliament and of the Council of 3 April 2014 on the freezing and confiscation of instrumentalities and proceeds of crime in the European Union*, https://eur-lex.europa.eu/eli/dir/2014/42/oj/eng. [4]

GRECO (2022), *Joint First and Second Evaluation Rounds Evaluation Report on Kazakhstan*, http://www.coe.int/greco. [11]

OECD (2024), *Baseline Report of the Fifth Round of Monitoring of Anti-Corruption Reforms in Kazakhstan the Istanbul Anti-Corruption Action Plan*, OECD, https://doi.org/10.1787/c9652173-en (accessed on 9 May 2025). [9]

OECD (2024), *Combatting High-level Corruption in Eastern Europe: Insights and Solutions*, OECD Publishing, Paris, https://doi.org/10.1787/3c82f87d-en. [2]

OECD (2023), *Istanbul Anti-Corruption Action Plan, 5th Round of Monitoring: Guide*, https://doi.org/10.1787/2ca61fcd-en. [12]

OECD (2020), *Fighting Corruption in Eastern Europe and Central Asia Anti-Corruption Reforms in Eastern Europe and Central Asia*, https://doi.org/10.1787/20743572. [18]

OECD (2017), *Anti-Corruption Reforms in Kazakhstan: 4th round of monitoring of the Istanbul Anti-Corruption Action Plan*, https://doi.org/10.1787/f6d3e193-en (accessed on 2 June 2025). [8]

OECD (2017), *OECD Integrity Scan of Kazakhstan: Preventing Corruption for a Competitive Economy*, OECD Public Governance Reviews, OECD Publishing, Paris, https://doi.org/10.1787/9789264272880-en. [19]

OECD (1997), *Convention on Combating Bribery of Foreign Public Officials in International Business Transactions And related documents*, https://legalinstruments.oecd.org/en/instruments/OECD-LEGAL-0293. [20]

President of the Republic of Kazakhstan (2025), *О мерах по совершенствованию системы государственного управления*, https://www.akorda.kz/ru/o-merah-po-sovershenstvovaniyu-sistemy-gosudarstvennogo-upravleniya-3051530 (accessed on 17 July 2025). [24]

Republic of Kazakhstan (2023), *On the return of illegally acquired assets to the state.* [10]

Republic of Kazakhstan (2014), *Code of Administrative Offences of the Republic of Kazakhstan*, https://adilet.zan.kz/eng/docs/K010000155_ (accessed on 2 June 2025). [22]

Republic of Kazakhstan (2014), "Criminal Code of the Republic of Kazakhstan". [5]

Republic of Kazakhstan (2014), *Criminal Procedure Code of the Republic of Kazakhstan*, https://adilet.zan.kz/eng/docs/Z970000206_ (accessed on 10 June 2025). [6]

Republic of Kazakhstan (2014), *Criminal Procedure Law of the Republic of Kazakhstan.* [25]

Republic of Kazakhstan (2008), "Budget Code of the Republic of Kazakhstan". [21]

Republic of Kazakhstan (1995), *Constitution of the Republic of Kazakhstan*, https://adilet.zan.kz/eng/docs/K950001000_ (accessed on 4 June 2025). [23]

Republic of Kazakhstan (1994), *Civil Code of the Republic of Kazakhstan*, https://adilet.zan.kz/eng/docs/K940001000_. [15]

Republic of Kazakhstan Supreme Court (2015), *On certain issues of imposing criminal punishment.* [14]

Republic of Moldova (2002), *Criminal Code.* [16]

United Nations (2004), *United Nations Convention Against Corruption*, http://www.unodc.org. [3]

Азаттык Азия (Azattyk Asia) (2025), *«Для отвода глаз». Что происходит с кампанией по возврату активов в Казахстан ("A smoke screen": What is happening with the asset recovery campaign in Kazakhstan).* [13]

Notes

[1] A term used in Kazakhstan to refer to ethnic Kazakhs who have returned to their historical homeland from abroad.

[2] The event and the elements of the criminal offense (time, place, method, and other circumstances of its commission), and the culpability of the individual for committing the offense, the form of their culpability, the motives and any legal or factual errors.

[3] It should be considered that the official statistics does not cover corruption in the private sector in the list of corruption offenses (Articles 250, 251 and 253 of the CC (2014[5])).

[4] By the Decree of the President of the Republic of Kazakhstan dated 30 June 2025 the Anti-Corruption Agency was reorganised through its merger into the National Security Committee of the Republic of Kazakhstan (2025[24]).

[5] Referring to cases where only the bribe-giver was prosecuted (under Article 367 of the CC - active bribery), cases where both a bribe-giver and a bribe-taker were prosecuted are not analysed in this section, since the proceeds of the crime (passive bribery) must be confiscated from the bribe-taker.

[6] In the criminal law of Kazakhstan, "theft" (хищение) is defined as the unlawful appropriation or conversion of another's property for personal gain, carried out without compensation, resulting in harm to the owner or other possessor of that property (Para 17 of Article 3 of the CC (2014[5])). Depending on the nature of the unlawful act, "theft" may manifest as larceny, fraud, robbery, embezzlement, misappropriation, etc. Para 3 Part 3 of Article 189 of the CC provides for liability for the misappropriation or embezzlement of property entrusted to the offender, committed by a person authorised to perform public functions, or a person equivalent to such, or by a public official, or by a person holding a responsible state position, if these acts are accompanied by the misuse of their official position.

[7] Criminal offenses are categorised into crimes and misdemeanours. A crime is a more severe form of a criminal offense. A misdemeanour poses lesser social danger, cause minor harm or create a threat of harm to individuals, organisations, society, or the state.

[8] Monthly calculation indicator was KZT 3 692 (approximately EUR 6 30) in 2024 and KZT 3 932 (approximately EUR 6 70) in 2025.

[9] At the time of drafting the study, the Parliament of Kazakhstan was considering amendments to the CC (Republic of Kazakhstan, 2014[5]), criminalising a promise and an offer of a bribe as autonomous offenses.

[10] The legislation of Kazakhstan distinguishes between the concepts of immunity and privileges from criminal prosecution, but both legal institutions provide guarantees against the conduct of criminal proceedings.

www.ingramcontent.com/pod-product-compliance
Lightning Source LLC
LaVergne TN
LVHW060454061126
851857LV00016B/1831
9789264597822